PRACTICE EDUCATION
IN SOCIAL WORK

Critical Skills
for Social Work

Pam **Field**
Cathie **Jasper**
Lesley **Littler**

Other books you might be interested in:

Anti-racism in Social Work Practice
Edited by Angie Bartoli   ISBN 978-1-909330-13-9

Modern Mental Health: Critical Perspectives on Psychiatric Practice
Edited by Steven Walker   ISBN 978-1-909330-53-5

Positive Social Work: The Essential Toolkit for NQSWs
By Julie Adams and Angie Sheard   ISBN 978-1-909330-05-4

Starting Social Work: Reflections of a Newly Qualified Social Worker
By Rebecca Joy Novell   ISBN 978-1-909682-

Evidencing CPD – A Guide to Building Your Social Work Portfo
By Daisy Bogg and Maggie Challis   ISBN 978-1-909330-25-2

Personal Safety for Social Workers and Health Professionals
By Brian Atkins   ISBN 978-1-909330-33-7

Understanding Substance Use: Policy and Practice
By Elaine Arnull   ISBN 978-1-909330-93-1

What's Your Problem? Making Sense of Social Problems and the Policy Process
By Stuart Connor   ISBN 978-1-909330-49-8

Titles are also available in a range of electronic formats. To order please go to our Website www.criticalpublishing.com or contact our distributor NBN International, 10 Thornbury Road, Plymouth PL6 7PP, telephone 01752 202301 or e-mail orders@ nbninternational.com

PRACTICE EDUCATION
IN SOCIAL WORK

Achieving Professional Standards

Critical Skills
for Social Work

Pam Field
Cathie Jasper
Lesley Littler

First published in 2014 by Critical Publishing Ltd.,

British Library Cataloguing in Publication Data
A CIP record for this book is available from the British Library

ISBN: 9781909330177

This book is also available in the following e-book formats:
Kindle ISBN: 9781909330184
EPUB ISBN: 9781909330191
Adobe e-book ISBN: 9781909330207

Cover design by Greensplash Limited
Project Management by Out of House Publishing
Typeset by Newgen Knowledge Works Pvt Ltd, India.
Printed and bound in Great Britain by Bell and Bain, Glasgow

Critical Publishing
152 Chester Road
Northwich
CW8 4AL

www.criticalpublishing.com

MIX
Paper from
responsible sources
FSC® C007785

Contents

Meet the authors

Pam Field is a registered social worker with a background in probation, youth offending and substance misuse work. Having become a Practice Educator in 1998, she was practice learning co-ordinator for a NW Borough Council from 2005–09, when she moved to the School of Social Work at UCLan as part of the Practice Learning Team. She is currently Senior Lecturer in Social Work and Work-based Learning Team Lead. She has been on the Committee of the National Organisation for Practice Teaching since 2007.

Cathie Jasper is a registered social worker and has practised with children and families, mainly with young people leaving care. While working as a practitioner, Cathie gained the Child Care Award and the Practice Teaching Award and was a Practice Educator of social work students. Since leaving direct social work practice, Cathie has been involved in the training of others, as a training officer for a NW local authority, a voluntary organisation, and as a member of MMU's social work department since 2009. She is currently a Senior Lecturer with responsibility for practice placements, the training of Practice Educators and more recently, with lead responsibility for the development of module provision and support for NQSWs undertaking their Assessed and Supported Year in Employment, and their supervisors. Cathie is the departmental representative on the Greater Manchester Practice Educator Programme Committee.

Lesley Littler is a registered social worker with a professional background in the Probation Service, Youth Offending and Family Court Welfare. Lesley has been a Practice Educator since 1986 and, whilst working in professional practice, took on the role of Specialist Practice Educator demonstrating her longstanding commitment to the professional development of others. She holds the Practice Teaching Award and is currently a Stage 2 Practice Educator. Lesley has worked in Higher Education for over 17 years in criminal justice, social work qualifying courses and the delivery of Practice Educator training. She is currently Senior Lecturer in Practice Learning at Edge Hill University.

Liz Munro is a registered social worker with a background in local authority fieldwork, having worked in both generic, and children and families social work teams. Liz gained experience of working as a Practice Educator for social work students while employed as a children and families social worker, and in 2004 was appointed as a University Lecturer (Practice Learning) and off-site Practice Educator for Salford University. She currently works as an Associate Lecturer for both Salford and Manchester Metropolitan Universities and as an off-site Practice Educator, Stage 2 Assessor and Second Opinion Practice Educator. Liz is a Practice Teaching Award holder and is also the current administrator for the National Organisation for Practice Teaching (NOPT).

Chapter 1 | Introduction and overview

Welcome and thank you for reading this book. This is a book for Practice Educators (PEs) in social work education. It offers guidance on the key skills and knowledge that PEs need in order to support and assess social work qualifying students, to enable their learning, and to manage their placements. It has been written by practising PEs, all of whom have the Practice Teaching Award (CCETSW, 1989) and who have been involved in Practice Education and developing and delivering Practice Education courses for a number of years.

The book was initially prompted by the pleasure and satisfaction the authors gained from teaching and delivering Practice Educator training courses and witnessing the enjoyment and learning that participants demonstrated. We wanted to ensure that such learning was nurtured and developed when the participants went back to their day jobs, as newly trained PEs and facing the responsibility for their first student. This book is meant to equip such PEs – to be a 'handy guide' to all that Practice Education and working with a student involves and a reminder (with a little more detail) of what they have covered in their initial Practice Education training course.

The emphasis in this book is thus on the *application* of key skills and knowledge embedded within the PE role; the *what* a PE needs to consider within the placement and the *how* of accomplishing it. Many of the theoretical considerations and objectives underpinning practice learning and education and the role of the PE that are mentioned in this book are covered in greater detail in other practice education texts, some of which are classics, and we have referred to them in this book. Please read these books for further insights and ideas as many of these texts cannot be bettered and remain as relevant to Practice Education today as when they were initially published.

A further prompt for this book has come from the more recent reforms to social work education in England as a result of the Social Work Task Force and the Social Work Reform Board (DfE, 2009; DfE, 2010); the development of The College of Social Work (TCSW) and new professional requirements embedded in the Professional Capabilities Framework (PCF) (TCSW, 2012b), and the *Practice Educator Professional Standards for Social Work (PEPS)* (TCSW, 2013b). As educators involved in practice learning, these reforms provided a motivation for us to revisit some of our ideas and thoughts about Practice Education and consider how the requirements would impact on the PE role and the expectations that would be placed on PEs as a result. Thus the 'handy guide' nature of this book also has another aspect – that of offering some helpful suggestions regarding the PE's preparation for their own assessment and how PEs might meet the learning outcomes of Domains A–D and the Values for Practice Educators and Supervisors and achieve Stage 1 and 2 of the PEPS (TCSW, 2013b).

While aimed primarily at those PEs who have just completed their training and who are putting into practice what they have learned with a student on placement (and are hoping to submit for Stage 1 of the *Practice Educator Professional Standards for Social Work* (TCSW, 2013b), the book will also be helpful for more experienced PEs. Such PEs may be submitting for Stage 2 of the PEPS (TCSW, 2013b) or may be involved in facilitating, supporting and assessing the professional development of post qualified practitioners such as Newly Qualified Social Workers (NQSWs). More experienced PEs may also view this book as a 'refresher' and it may be helpful for them in considering the requirements of the Professional Capabilities Framework (TCSW, 2012b) and the PEPS (TCSW, 2013b) in maintaining and developing their practice.

You may be reading this introduction and overview before reading other chapters in the book, or you may have dipped into and used the book and are reading this at a later point. However you are using this book, this introduction and overview will inform you of the structure of each chapter and an explanation of terms used to help your navigation.

Structure of each chapter

» Each chapter will begin with a reference to the *Practice Educator Professional Standards for Social Work (PEPS)* (TCSW, 2013b) and will outline how the content of that chapter links to the PEPS (TCSW, 2013b) and the Learning Outcome Domains required for Stage 1 and Stage 2.

» *Chapter aims* – each chapter will indicate the aims for the chapter.

» *Critical questions* – at the beginning of each chapter some key 'critical questions' will be outlined. These critical questions are the 'philosophical' questions that a critically reflective PE will be asking themselves throughout their reading of the chapter and during their practice. They encapsulate some of the challenges, dilemmas and complexities of the PE role in relation to the subject covered in the chapter.

» Within the chapter, there will be a mixture of the following.

Professional development prompts – These are reflective activities that the PE can carry out on their own or with a colleague. They act as a 'note to self' and are about issues and aspects of the PE role to consider in more depth and detail.

Exercise – These are exercises that a PE can undertake with a student.

Case example – For illustrative purposes.

» *What does the research say?* Where there is related research or one or two small research studies that have been carried out about an aspect of practice learning relevant to the subject covered in the chapter this section will outline the key messages highlighted in the research.

» *Taking it further* – This will indicate helpful further reading and include book/chapter references with brief details of content and particular areas covered.

Practice Education – where we are now

The book has been written in a period of change for social work and Practice Education in England, brought about by the changes recommended by the Social Work Task Force (DfE, 2009) and the Social Work Reform Board (DfE, 2010; SWRB, 2011a). The reference to 'achieving professional standards' within the title of the book acknowledges and refers to these changes. The reforms and the professional standards referred to in the following pages relate to requirements for social work education, training and registration in England. Different requirements exist for the other UK countries.

Social work reform and the PCF

The Social Work Reform Board originally developed the Professional Capabilities Framework (PCF) (TCSW, 2012b). It is now managed by TCSW and is the overarching framework of standards and professional development in social work. The PCF is divided into nine domains of practice/capability and nine levels of the social work career ladder – from entry to training as a social worker; the level students should be at the point of leaving university; after their first year of practice; at social worker, experienced social worker and advanced practitioner level; and at the strategic social work level. The PCF is a progressive framework – the capability levels relate to the knowledge, understanding and complexity of work that someone at that level in their career would be expected to manage, and progression between levels is determined by the practitioner's increasing abilities to manage issues such as complexity, risk and responsibility in a range of professional settings.

The PCF is represented as a 'rainbow' or a 'fan' – see overleaf – each 'colour' corresponding to one of the nine areas of capability:

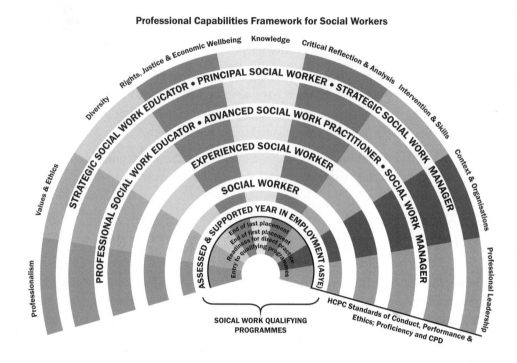

The levels relating to student social workers are of particular interest to PEs. These represent the 'level' of capability a social work student should be demonstrating at different points in their social work training.

> » By *the end of the first placement* students should demonstrate effective use of knowledge, skills and commitment to core values in social work in a given setting in predominantly less complex situations, with supervision and support. They will have demonstrated capacity to work with people and situations where there may not be simple clear-cut solutions.

> » By *the end of last placement/the completion of qualifying programmes* Newly Qualified Social Workers should have demonstrated the knowledge, skills and values to work with a range of user groups, and the ability to undertake a range of tasks at a foundation level; the capacity to work with more complex situations; they should be able to work more autonomously while recognising that the final decision will still rest with their supervisor; they will seek appropriate support and supervision (TCSW 2012c).

Progression between levels is characterised by development of the student's ability to manage complexity, risk, ambiguity and increasingly autonomous decision making across a range of situations and within each of the nine domains.

There have also been changes to the *placement structure* brought about within the reforms, and not only will all students be assessed under the PCF but the 200 days of practice learning will be as follows:

» 30 days skills development training, delivered within the university, across the degree course;

» first placement – 70 days;

» final placement – 100 days.

It is expected that placements are different at first and final level, ensuring that the student is provided with a broad, generic experience and to ensure that students have experience of different service user groups; different types of tasks in terms of the approaches and methods employed at the placement setting; and experience of different levels of complexity and professional autonomy between the first and final level placement. Further, the final placement should prepare students for the statutory aspects of social work, although this is defined by the nature of tasks involved rather than the setting (TCSW, 2012e).

The *Practice Educator Professional Standards for Social Work* (2013b)

The PEPS outline two stages of professional development and progression for PEs, which are minimum requirements that have come fully into effect from October 2013. The PEPS outline the two stages as 'commensurate with the different levels of responsibility in teaching, assessing and supervising social work degree students' (TCSW, 2013b) and describe the two stages as:

Stage 1. Practice Educators will be able to supervise, teach and assess social work students on a first placement. From October 2015, Practice Educators must be qualified and registered social workers.

Stage 2. Practice Educators will be able to supervise, teach and assess students up to and including the last placement and the point of qualification. Stage 2 Practice Educators must be qualified and registered social workers.

The PEPS (TCSW, 2013b) are national requirements that define the knowledge, skills and values that PEs need to demonstrate at Stage 1 and 2, and which are outlined within Domains A–D and the Values for Practice Educators and Supervisors. Local and regional partnerships can decide how PEs can demonstrate and meet the domains requirements and learning outcomes outlined at each stage. There must be guidance and support available to PEs who are undertaking Stage 1 and 2 from an appropriately qualified mentor (who must be Stage 2 qualified). When undertaking Stage 1 and Stage 2, PEs must also be observed in their practice with a student *teaching, supervising and assessing against the PCF* (TCSW, 2013b) and this must be carried out by a Stage 2 qualified, registered social worker. Reference will be made to the PE's own observation of their practice in Chapter 9.

Health and Care Professions Council (HCPC)

Since 2012 the HCPC has been the regulating body for social workers in England. The HCPC defines the standards that social workers must meet and adhere to in order to register and remain registered with the HCPC and be considered fit to practise as a social worker. The HCPC states that these are:

> » HCPC Standards of Proficiency (SOPS) – These are the threshold standards necessary for safe and effective practice within the profession. They set out what a social worker in England must know, understand and be able to do following the completion of their social work degree;

> » HCPC Standards of Conduct, Performance and Ethics;

> » Standards for continuing professional development (CPD).

The HCPC does not register student social workers. However, students are expected to conduct themselves in accordance with HCPC *Guidance on conduct and ethics for students.*

How do these reforms and professional requirements affect PEs?

These various reforms and professional requirements will affect PEs in a number of ways and they are mentioned throughout the book.

> » All Practice Educators, newly qualified or otherwise, are required to assess prequalifying social work students according to the relevant domains of the PCF and to make holistic judgements about a student's progress and development while on a first or final placement (TCSW, 2012a). This requirement affects all PEs, and thus PEs – 'newer' and 'older' alike – are currently learning together about this requirement and how it affects their role and the assessment of social work students. All of the chapters in this book make

reference to the requirements of the PCF as they relate to the support and assessment of social work students at first and final placement level.

» The PCF is relevant to PEs not only because it is the developmental framework within which they support and assess social work students, but also because it is the framework within which all social workers operate and progress and the role of PE can play a part in this progression. Thus, at Social Worker and Experienced Social Worker levels, Domain 9 requires that practitioners contribute to the learning of others and assess and manage students. For some employers it is a requirement of progression that social workers undertake PE training and become PEs; for other employers the role of PE/assessor/mentor is specifically written into job descriptions. The particular requirements regarding PEs' CPD are outlined in Chapter 9.

» The PEPS (TCSW, 2013b) require that PEs are assessed at either or both Stages 1 and 2 and that PEs maintain their currency once they have achieved these stages, in line with HCPC requirements for re-registration. There are references to the requirements of the PEPS (TCSW, 2013b) and what PEs need to do to meet these requirements at Stage 1 and 2 throughout the book.

» HCPC requirements outline that social workers re-register every two years and provide evidence of their Continuing Professional Development (CPD). Undertaking the PE role is an example of CPD which can be recorded within the social worker's 'scope of practice' as evidence of development of their skills and knowledge and their ongoing ability to practise effectively as a social worker.

Practice Education – how we got here

There is a long history of practice learning and education in the UK. As far back as 1967, Priscilla Young's book on *The Student and Supervision in Social Work Education* explained the role of the supervisor on placement as teacher, planner, administrator and assessor of the placement and 'helper' to the student, speaking of similar functions of Practice Education as we do today. Since that time, Practice Education has been the subject of many changes – in name, function and route of accreditation.

The term 'student supervisor' was replaced by 'Practice Teacher' and an enhanced educational purpose designated within the requirements of the Practice Teacher Award (CCETSW, 1989); later, the term 'Practice Assessor' was introduced and used with the introduction of social work degree (DoH, 2002); and more recently, the term Practice Educator has been used (TCSW, 2013b). The Practice Teacher Award was replaced by the revised PQ Framework (GSCC, 2005) which included post qualifying awards at progressive levels of specialism. The first 'specialist' level incorporated a module in 'enabling others' which required candidates to develop skills and knowledge in enabling the learning and development of others. However, in 2009, the Draft Practice Educator Framework (SfC, 2009) was published, consultation on which has resulted in the PEPS (TCSW, 2013b).

The introduction of the PEPS (TCSW, 2013b) has once again promoted Practice Education as a 'stand-alone' award and achievement, thus giving it, some would say, the prominence and recognition it deserves. However, the PEPS (TCSW, 2013b) is part of the wider reforms to social work and is accompanied by an emphasis on the necessity for an improved teaching and learning culture within agencies to enhance effective social work practice (Munro, 2011). There is also a focus on supporting staff in their Continuing Professional Development (DfE, 2009) and the acknowledgement that social work students require high quality practice placements that provide skilled and professional *supervision, guidance and assessment* (DfE, 2009, p. 20). The SWTF Final Report (DfE, 2009) suggested that, to achieve this, employers should support Practice Educators in their *on-going learning and development* and in the development of their skills *as part of their responsibility for investing in the next generation of social workers* (DfE, 2009, p. 24).

Conclusion

We believe PEs play an important part in helping to develop the next generation of social workers and this book is written to assist PEs in the development of skills and knowledge that will help them achieve this task. We hope PEs find this book helpful in informing their practice with students. We would therefore welcome the feedback of PEs who have used this book and the exercises and ideas within it; we would also welcome any suggestions for additions to chapters.

We wish you all the best in the teaching and learning endeavour of Practice Education.

The material in this chapter links to the following PEPS domains and values statements for PEs and supervisors:

Additional learning outcome required for Stage 2 PEs

B:10

Values for PEs and supervisors: 1–7

Chapter aims

» To examine key relevant frameworks of values and ethics.

» To assist the PE in teaching and assessing values with their students in the context of professional practice.

» To consider the power relationship between the PE and student and the role of anti-oppressive practice.

Critical **questions**

» How do I allow for the uniqueness and diversity of learners' viewpoints while upholding the core values of social work (Value 3 (PEPS, 2013b))?

» How do I assess in a manner that does not disadvantage learners while ensuring standards of the profession are upheld (Value 5 (PEPS, 2013b))?

» How do I ensure that the teaching of values is integrated with other aspects of practice?

Introduction

Social workers are required to adhere to the HCPC Standards of Conduct, Performance and Ethics (2012b) and are also required by the PCF to demonstrate that they can conduct themselves ethically and use social work ethics and values to guide their professional practice (Domain 2). Professional bodies such as TCSW have published a Code of Ethics (2013); the British Association of Social Workers (BASW) 2012) has an updated and lengthy Code of Ethics for Social Work; and The International Federation of Social Workers has a Statement of Ethical Principles (2012). The PEPS (TCSW, 2013b) contain the Values for Practice Educators and Supervisors and outline how PEs should promote anti-oppressive and anti-discriminatory practice in the assessment of students.

Practice Education is not a simple undertaking. It involves challenge and complexity – on a personal and practical level it demands the negotiation and management of interpersonal relationships between the PE and student, within wider contexts, environments and regulations that are ever-changing. It involves the PE in roles as manager, enabler, facilitator, supervisor, assessor, teacher, supporter, negotiator, planner, mediator – and probably more in these testing times. Thus, the multi-layered and sometimes contested nature of each of these roles means that Practice Education is and has to be a 'thinking' enterprise. Within each of these roles – and at many stages of their deployment – PEs will be challenged in their practice and will have to critically reflect upon it. This will inevitably encompass thinking about how they are practising ethically and with sound values at the core. Each chapter in this book assists PEs in this process and invites you to think about your practice through asking yourselves 'critical questions' and using 'professional development prompts'.

When writing this book we gave considerable thought as to whether there should be a separate chapter on 'Values and ethics'. We are aware that the recent social work reforms (DfE, 2009; DfE, 2010; SWRB, 2011) led to the development of a professional framework (PCF) which has sought to define social work practice in a way which makes the awareness and application of values implicit. Values and ethics underpin practice in a way that makes it impossible to view the PCF domains discretely – a sea change from the previous qualifying assessment standards, the National Occupational Standards (NOS) (TOPSS, England 2002a). Professional practice cannot be undertaken without all elements being present. The nine domains are interactive; they work together to describe the knowledge, skills and values that social workers need to practise effectively. (TCSW, 2012d).

In the same way, social work ethics and values are integral to the whole endeavour of Practice Education and their consideration must therefore permeate the practice of PEs and inform the processes of enabling, supporting and assessing learning. PEs and students should be discouraged from regarding 'values' or 'anti-oppressive practice' as aspects that stand alone within their practice or in discussions.

In addition to this, the relationship between PE and learner is infused with power differentials and raises the question of anti-oppressive practice within the PE– student relationship. Therefore, adherence to social work values and ethics is expected and assumed, and underpins the material and discussion within each chapter in the book. This chapter will partly serve to signpost the reader to discussions in later chapters.

Despite the acknowledgment that values and ethics are *implicit* within practice, at the same time their consideration is made *explicit* by the very inclusion in the PCF of the domains 'values and ethics' and 'diversity'. Additional Codes of Ethics in existence also direct us to consider these aspects of our practice separately.

The authors therefore decided that we would reflect the explicit/implicit dichotomy by including a chapter on 'values and ethics' that is to be taken in addition to the material to be found throughout the book as a whole.

The objectives of the chapter are:

» to defuse anxiety often associated with the teaching and assessment of values and ethics;

» to enable PEs and students to understand more fully the contribution of underpinning values and ethics to a holistic approach to practice and assessment;

» to give due weight to the values statements in the PEPS (TCSW, 2013b).

The chapter reminds the reader of the values frameworks currently relevant to social work and the PE role. It explores how the PE can educate and support students to develop their professional value base and guide them through the ethical dimensions of their work. Consideration is given to the acknowledgment and management of power dynamics within the educator–student relationship. Exercises and professional development prompts are offered to enable the reader to develop and self-evaluate their approach with students and ensure that they fully consider and meet the PEPS values statements as required. The aim is thus to promote anti-oppressive practice education and the promotion of anti-oppressive and ethical practice in students.

Before commencing placement students will have had some teaching about social work values and ethics. Given that the terms are sometimes confused or used interchangeably it might be helpful as a practice-based educator to discuss your student's understanding and ensure that they have a clear idea about what values underpin social work and how ethical principles and codes of ethics and conduct have grown from, and embody, those values.

The BASW Code of Ethics (revised 2012) gives helpful definitions, defining social work values as beliefs which people find particularly valuable in a social work context – this extends to the desirable character traits of people engaged in the profession. *Values are based on respect for the equality, worth, and dignity of all people* (BASW, 2012). Ethics are defined as relating to right or wrong conduct in a professional context. The Code comprises statements of values and ethical principles relating to human rights, social justice and professional integrity, followed by practice principles that indicate how the ethical principles should be applied in practice.

Frameworks of values and ethics for social workers: reform

A key challenge following the recent social work reforms (DfE, 2009 DfE, 2010; SWRB, 2011) has been the redevelopment of a cohesive framework around ethics and values, given the split responsibility for regulation and registration (HCPC) and professional guidance (TCSW). Previously the functions of regulation, registration and provision of professional standards via a Code of Practice were all held by one body (the General Social Care Council (GSCC)). Moreover, National Occupational Standards (TOPSS, 2002a) contained a set of values statements that formed part of the Statement of Expectations developed by people who used services and their carers, and hence were felt by many involved in social work practice and education to represent authority and authenticity. These values statements directly informed the GSCC Code of Practice and could be used alongside it to teach and assess social work students. Their essential components were:

» respect for service users and carers;

» empowerment of service users and carers;

» honesty about power and resources;

» confidentiality and its limits;

» challenging discrimination.

Frameworks now in use can be seen to encompass preceding guidance, with some expansion. For example, the core values that higher education institutions (HEIs) are required to meet for endorsement of their social work courses by TCSW closely reflect the GSCC values statements. These are: valuing diversity, challenging our own prejudices, maintaining probity and integrity, preventing and challenging discrimination, reflecting on our own practice, and working inclusively (TCSW, 2012g). It can be seen that these are key for educators both in universities and in practice learning settings.

Current frameworks for all social workers

The PCF (TCSW)

The PCF has social work values and ethics embedded throughout its nine domains, with two in particular – 'values and ethics' (Domain 2) and 'diversity' (Domain 3) – requiring a more explicit focus on this area of capability. It is interesting to note the introduction of a domain requiring social workers to apply knowledge and understanding of broader human rights principles including international law (Domain 4 'Rights, Justice and Economic Wellbeing'). This represents an advancement of social and political awareness and engagement more akin to the internationally agreed *Definition of Social Work* (The International Federation of Social Workers (IFSW, 2012) and The International Association of Schools of Social Work (IASSW), 2012). This definition is explicit within BASW's Code of Ethics, reflected in a commitment to human rights and social justice.

The Standards of Proficiency (SOPS) (HCPC)

Values and ethics are also to be found integrated into the SOPS which are standards of proficiency for social work required by the HCPC for registration – social work students have to demonstrate that they meet these standards by the end of their training. Final placements therefore are key in ensuring these are demonstrated by students in practice. They have been mapped against the PCF (TCSW 2012f) to ensure that there is consistency and a shared understanding.

Standards of conduct, performance and ethics (HCPC)

The HCPC Standards replace the GSCC Code of Practice for social workers. As the HCPC does not register students, there are two versions of these standards:

1. *Standards of conduct, performance and ethics* (HCPC) which lay out *duties as a registrant*;

2. *Guidance on conduct and ethics for students* (HCPC) is generally followed by HEIs and throughout training. It is likely that you will be required to assess your student against these standards.

Additional frameworks

Two further Codes of Ethics are available for social workers for reference.

1. BASW *Code of Ethics* (2012) – Produced for its members and providing a comprehensive discussion of the definitions of values, ethics and practice principles with a helpful guide to behaviours representing professional ethical practice.

2. TCSW (2013a) *Code of Ethics for Membership of the College of Social Work* – This document expresses its non-mandatory function of ensuring professional standards alongside the mandatory requirements of the HCPC *Standards of conduct, performance and ethics*. It comprises a set of principles of professional standards, with related values and behaviours explored in a sub-statement.

Additional frameworks for PEs and supervisors

Values for Practice Educators and supervisors (PEPS 2013b)

Originally developed as the values for social care work-based assessors by the GSCC (TOPSS, 2002b), these now represent the values for PEs to be demonstrated alongside Domains A–D in submission for Stage 1 or 2 status. The seven values statements can be summarised as four core themes.

1. The Continuing Professional Development of the educator and application of knowledge to the assessment process.

2. The use of authority and power, including considering own prejudices and personal values.

3. Respect for the individual needs and preferences of students.

4. Anti-oppressive practice within the assessment process.

It is important to note that although these are presented as generic values statements, they largely relate to the assessment function.

NOPT (National Organisation for Practice Teaching) Code of Practice (revised in 2013)

Intended as *a statement of the principles through which the role of the practice educator and the task of practice teaching is discharged* (NOPT, 2013), this Code of Practice was developed by NOPT members and is available on their Website for reference.

Gaining a sense of cohesion around the co-existing, complementary values and ethics frameworks may be difficult for students and PEs alike. Nevertheless Domain 2 of the PCF (*Values and Ethics: Apply social work ethical principles and values to guide professional practice*) requires that social workers are *knowledgeable about the value base of their profession, its ethical standards and relevant law.* Your role as PE is to make sure that students gain a clear sense of their professional underpinning values and ethics as well as locating their practice within the HCPC Standards of Conduct and Ethics, and ensuring that it is in line to meet with the SOPS at the point of qualification.

The following exercise may be helpful to complete with your student if you feel they are lacking a sense of the professional value base.

> ### Exercise
>
> Ask your student to read and compare a selection of the key standards and codes of ethics as laid out previously. Ask them to present in supervision:
>
> » their understanding of the most commonly expressed values;
>
> » their understanding of key ethical principles;
>
> » some examples of behaviours that illustrate those principles.
>
> Subsequently you could work with your student in analysing a piece of their own work with these values and ethical principles in mind.

Educating about values

It is hoped that the exercise described above will help you, as PE, understand your role in helping students develop their understanding of their own personal values, the professional underpinning values of social work, and how these are translated into practice. The focus is thus not on 'teaching' values, but on assisting students to become aware of their own value base and how it aligns to the professional value base they will be required to demonstrate and put into practice.

Recognising and managing the impact of values on the PE's work with a student (Value 1 (PEPS))

The raising of awareness of one's values and beliefs, and their impact on practice, is a fundamental expectation of social work education. Learning to understand the role that values play in their social work practice is a significant aspect of placement for students, and often one of the most challenging. This can be an area where students feel at their most vulnerable and require support. The power differential between PE and student can be heightened as students fear that revealing 'wrong' values may impair their ability to be assessed positively; conversely, a PE may feel that their views and practice are under scrutiny. For a PE the conflicts that arise daily in practice will be thrown into relief through the challenge of exploring them with a student, and enhanced by the complexities of the PE role. Both parties may thus challenge and question each other. In order to maximise the potential for constructive debate and education, honest discussion is essential and a climate needs to be established in which sometimes difficult areas of assumptions, prejudices, values, beliefs and ethical questions can be examined, reflected upon and accommodated into professional development. The PE must be as prepared as the student to explore such issues honestly. Chapter 5 on supervision will explore how honesty and sharing of power can be established within the supervisory relationship. In addition some of the tools introduced in Chapter 6 on assessment to promote holistic social work practice and assessment will include prompts to such discussions.

In order to prepare for work on this potentially intimate level with your student, it is important that you as PE do not lose sight of the relationship between personal values and professional practice, and that you enable your student to contextualise this. It can be helpful to remind yourself of the different 'values systems' that can apply within social work practice. These can be broken down into the personal, professional, organisational and societal for the purpose of exploring them with a student. (Maclean and Caffrey, 2009).

Professional **development prompt**

Think about the personal values you hold.

» How did they inform your decision to become a social worker?

» How do they inform your practice as a PE?

» Think of examples of how your personal values might (or do) conflict in practice with the professional, organisational and societal values you encounter in the context of your practice as a social worker and as a PE.

» You may wish to initiate a discussion with your student using the same prompts.

The importance of critically reflective practice cannot be overstated at this point. As we will see throughout the book, the development of the skill of self-awareness and self-knowledge, and understanding of the impact of self on others, is key to the development and assessment of a student (Values 1, 7). Chapter 8 will assist you in developing a critically reflective approach to values and ethics alongside other aspects of social work practice.

Assessing values – opportunities to demonstrate capability

In order to assess the inclusion of appropriate values and ethical understanding it is important that you as PE provide opportunities for the student to explore, question and understand the relevant issues, and to demonstrate how they inform their practice.

In preparation you may wish to begin to analyse your own practice setting as follows:

Professional **development prompt**

Think of one core task undertaken in your placement setting (eg initial assessment/care plan/report for Core Group meeting) in preparation for working with a student.

» Examine the organisational values that inform the task.

» Examine HCPC Standards that may apply when you carry out the task. Note the personal values that become relevant for you.

The importance of planning appropriate learning opportunities for students is discussed elsewhere in the book, and at various points you will find other suggestions of ways in which to promote exploration and development of appropriate values and ethical practice.

Assisting a student in developing the appropriate skills base

It is not unusual for students to struggle with reflection and articulating their own value base. It is well acknowledged that social work education can induce significant questioning of personal beliefs and values and that this, combined with the harsh realities of contemporary social work practice, can lead to a sense of confusion and lack of clarity.

You may find the following exercise helpful as a non-threatening way of assisting your student to begin to examine their own assumptions and beliefs. You could also give examples from your own experience of socialisation.

Exercise

Ask your student the following questions:

» Look back to your childhood. What were you encouraged to believe about older people/people with mental health difficulties/young offenders (substitute the relevant service user group) and their role in society?

» Who influenced your beliefs?

» Have your beliefs changed? If so, how and why?

(Adapted from Maclean and Caffrey, 2009)

To help students make the connection between their personal beliefs and professional practice, this exercise can be developed into a 'personal review', as follows:

Exercise: **ask your student**

Imagine that in your social work role you are preparing to interview the following (these can be adapted according to the setting):

1. an older person and their carer who are reluctantly considering admission to a residential care setting;

2. a young man aged 16 who is to appear in court on a charge of demanding money with menaces from children in the neighbourhood;

3. a man who has a recurrence of a depressive illness;

4. a woman who reports an incidence of domestic violence.

In order to ensure that you can effectively put yourself in their shoes.

» Conduct a *personal and cultural review* of yourself; that is, an enquiry into what your experiences (direct and indirect) have been in relation to the issues raised in these scenarios. For example, in relation to the first scenario: Who have I cared for? How would I feel about being cared for by a relative? How do I use my free time? How do I react when I cannot do what I want? What balance do I like to draw between my time and time with my family?

» Now frame some questions, informed by these personal values, which will best gain relevant information from these service users and help you to assist them in your professional role.

(Adapted from Shaw, 1997, in Beverley and Worsley, 2007, p. 95)

Exercises such as those above can help a student to 'tune in' to service users' perspectives, a crucial first step in demonstrating care and respect in undertaking an intervention. In turn, discussions based on these types of exercises can help you as PE assess a student's progress and learning needs.

Conclusion

This chapter will have helped you in thinking about the place of values and ethics in practice and how anti-oppressive principles should frame the teaching, support and assessment activities with a student. Many of the prompts and exercises can be used by the PE to raise their own self-awareness before they begin to work with a student.

Further chapters, dealing with particular areas of PE practice, will offer more material regarding the operation of values and ethics that the PE can use and reflect upon.

Taking it further

Banks, S. (2012, 4th ed.) *Ethics and Values in Social Work*, Basingstoke: Palgrave Macmillan. A well established book on this topic. The introduction and Chapter 2 in particular are useful in looking at the difference between values and ethics, and considering the role of the social worker politically and ethically in society. Useful case studies illustrate the arguments put forward.

Thompson, N. (2009, 3rd ed.) *Understanding Social Work*, Basingstoke: Palgrave Macmillan. This is a book that students are likely to be reading. Chapter 5 explores the value base of social work with a particular emphasis on skills needed to apply and integrate values effectively.

Maclean, S. and Caffrey, B. (2009) *Developing a Practice Curriculum*, Rugeley: Kirwin Maclean Associates Ltd. This book approaches the task of working with your student on values and ethics practically, with useful exercises and prompts for discussion.

Chapter 3 | Preparation, planning and induction

The material in this chapter links to the following PEPS domains and values statements for PEs and supervisors:

Learning outcome domains required for Stage 1 and Stage 2 PEs

Domain A; B:2; B:3; B:4; B:6; B:7; B:10

Additional learning outcome domains required for Stage 2 PEs

D:1; D:2

Values for PEs and supervisors: 1, 3–7

Chapter aims

- » To review good practice principles in preparing and planning for a social work student placement.

- » To consider the involvement of service users and colleagues in the preparation and planning process.

- » To consider how to meet individual student needs with a focus on planning an appropriate learning curriculum.

Critical **questions**

- » Who am I as a practitioner, as a learner, as a PE?

- » How can I present my organisation as a service provider and as a focus for good practice and a learning organisation?

- » How can I ensure the application of the value base of the PEPS?

Introduction

As Williams and Rutter (2010) note, *planning and preparation should ideally start at the moment you first consider the possibility of providing support for learning in your workplace* (p. 31). This chapter will begin from this premise, looking first at what the PE may think through before they actually meet the student. Later in the chapter we will reflect on the issues surrounding the arrival of the student.

Before meeting the student

Before meeting the student there are a number of critical issues that the PE will wish to consider. Thinking 'externally' – looking inside from the outside – of the organisation in which they are deployed or related to, the PE will need to contemplate how both they and a prospective student may appraise the agency as a learning organisation, a focus for good practice and, of course, as a service provider. In turn this will promote more 'internal' reflections for the PE – who am I as a practitioner, as a learner, as an educator? These are challenging questions, making deep connections to one's value base and that of the profession – including the values located within the PEPS.

Knowing the course, knowing your responsibilities

As a PE it is vital that you develop a working knowledge of the relevant social work course requirements including, especially, the framework for the assessment of placements and the expectations related to your role. However, these responsibilities take place in a shifting context and PEs need to be aware of the broader environment in which Practice Education takes place. It is essential therefore to understand how recent changes have influenced our approach to social work education and in particular Practice Education and learning. A core principle behind the ideas presented in this chapter is that practice learning takes place both in the university and the workplace, and this chapter will encourage you to think about how to bridge the gap between work-based learning and academic learning. This is a key principle of the Social Work Reform Board's (SWRB, 2009, 2011) recommendations, and manifested in the Professional Capability Framework (PCF), which has been designed on the basis of continuous, career-long professional development.

A further principle of the SWRB recommendations, detailed in the document *Effective Partnership Working* (SWRB, 2011b), has been the emphasis on partnership working so that academic learning is not isolated from practice learning as it may have been in the past. This document emphasises the importance of universities (HEIs), employers and service users and carers working together to deliver a whole social work education programme as partners in an educative process that leads to the social work professional qualification.

One of the interesting and perhaps more radical shifts recommended by the SWRB was the change made to the number of placement days – a reduction from a minimum of 200 to 170 days. The intention of this move is to embed skills development more into academic programmes in readiness for placements. This is partly in response to common complaints from PEs and host agencies in the past that students were not prepared for 'real life' practice and were often lacking core basic skills. Ironically, this change means students will have less 'real life' practice than before. Thus, from 2013, 30 days will have to be identified by universities specifically as skills development days, which are to be facilitated and delivered by a combination of academic staff, practitioners, service users and carers. This is an interesting development which will require universities to work closely with local partners in ensuring effective outcomes for students. In addition to the skills development days there is also a specific require-ment under arrangements for Endorsement by TCSW for universities to ensure that their students have been assessed under criteria located within the PCF, for *Readiness for Direct Practice* before their first placement. While social work programmes have had a similar expectation in the past, this assessment must now be carried out by a combination of academic staff, social workers and service users and carers – and is a welcome broadening of the process into the partnerships (TCSW, 2012l).

Involvement of social workers and PEs within the university learning programme enhances and refreshes student and staff awareness and knowledge of current practice, as well as preparing students for the reality of current practice which they will experi-ence once on placement. For PEs, contributing to this development for students would help you achieve capability within the PCF Domain 9 (***Professional Leadership***).

There has been a shift to seeking national consistency in placement provision and prac-tice learning with the development of requirements and recommendations for prin-ciples and outcomes in university-based learning, practice learning and the Assessed and Supported Year in Employment (ASYE). One of the most important changes is from the previous framework of National Occupational Standards (TOPSS, 2002) to a notion of holistic assessment set against the PCF and informed by two important doc-uments outlining the expectations of the new professional body, the Health and Care Professions Council (HCPC); namely the Standards of Education and Training (SETs) (HCPC, 2012e) – which outline what is expected *generically* of all professional quali-fying programmes approved by the HCPC – and the Standards of Proficiency (SOPS) (HCPC, 2012a) – which detail the standards students must specifically have achieved by the end of professional training to enable their registration with the HCPC. It is the notion of holistic assessment that perhaps carries the most significant shift for PEs and students on placement with them:

Holistic assessment is used where learning or performance objectives are inter-related and complex and the extent of learning or performance is measured against established standards. This approach is particularly relevant to social work, especially now that standards have been set at different career levels through the Professional Capabilities Framework (PCF) – the development of professional judgement and expertise can be assessed as a whole to reflect the complexity of social work practice. Throughout their career, social work students and practitioners need to demonstrate integration of all aspects of learning, including knowledge and experience in terms of the PCF, and be able to generalise and transfer their learning to untaught applications.

(TCSW, 2012m, p. 1)

We will address holistic assessment in much more detail in Chapter 6.

Your preparation as a PE should therefore include knowledge of what the students are doing at university as well as, where possible, actively seeking to participate in their practice learning within university. In addition to an awareness of the national guidelines you will need to have knowledge of the individual university course requirements. You may work for an organisation that provides placements to students from a range of universities who may all have different requirements within the overall framework. Make sure you receive information from the university as to their documentation, assessment requirements, procedural structures and expectations of PEs. Some regions have harmonised approaches and documentation in order to provide more consistency for PEs.

Understanding the roles and responsibilities of a PE

There are many ways of supporting or enabling learning in the workplace – mentoring qualified colleagues through their Continuing Professional Development is one example – and the new emphasis on developmental and incremental progress through a career using the PCF implies that work-based enablers will be needed at all stages: this specifically meets Domain D:6 (*Demonstrate an ability to transfer PE skills, knowledge and values to new roles in mentoring, supervision, teaching and/or assessment*). Here are a number of examples of where PEs might seek evidence against Domain 6 in their role:

> » social work students – to provide input and assessment on courses and during placement;

- » NQSWs during ASYE – to supervise and assess NQSWs against ASYE outcomes;

- » colleagues undertaking post qualifying Continuing Professional Development – supervising, mentoring and undertaking direct observations of practice;

- » induction of new staff;

- » mentoring or coaching;

- » supervision;

- » participating in or facilitating team-based learning events.

Chapter 9 will explore these roles further.

The latter three roles outlined above have become more significant recently, as workplaces appear to have, in some cases, lost their cohesion as they have introduced more flexible working arrangements. Practical arrangements are key here – many of us now work in an 'agile' environment where working from home or a hub, 'touching down' and 'hot desking' is the norm. How are you going to manage this environment and mode of working with a student? There are innovative methods emerging – team meetings, peer supervision and safety arrangements involving daily briefings. This can be a very disruptive and insecure environment for a student. You need to think about how you can encourage the student placed with you to adapt to this environment and work positively within it.

Preparation of self

Once you have an understanding of the context in which practice education is taking place, before your student arrives it is vital to prepare yourself. The PEPS provide a framework to detail the roles/activities and responsibilities of a PE, and also take a developmental approach, with Domains A, B and C being required to be evidenced for Stage 1, and Domain D needing to be evidenced for Stage 2.

On a purely practical level you need to ensure that your own workload is planned and organised in a way which is conducive to hosting a social work student placement. If you work part time, or have a flexible working pattern, you will need to think about your time management and maintaining accountability and availability for your student. Is there an agreement for PEs in your agency which makes clear whether you may expect any workload relief or other support?

It may be helpful to think of your preparation in terms of thinking about your knowledge, skills, values and strengths. If this is your first student, reflect on what you can draw on from your role as a social worker to help you develop skills in enabling learning that will apply to a student. When your student arrives, you may well consider looking at their learning style. It is important that you also know what your own learning (and teaching) style is, in order to be able to construct a programme of learning and teaching that stretches you and provides a comprehensive experience for a student. Learning styles and their uses will be explored in Chapter 4.

If you have had a student before, and are perhaps also working towards Stage 2, you will need to look at your development – in order to meet Domain D and the values statements. For example, you may need to improve and broaden your supervision skills to evidence Domain B:10. Chapter 5 looks at this in more detail.

It is important to understand the many and various roles of a PE. The following exercise may be helpful in beginning to think about this:

Professional **development prompt**

What activities do you undertake as a PE? What functions do they relate to?

Function	Support	Education	Management
Activities			

(Taken from Morrison, 1993)

PEs we have trained have found this useful in helping them analyse, on a practical level, the functions they are required to embody and perform as a PE, and vital in ensuring they are prepared for possible eventualities. To take them one by one:

Support

Students have the right to practise in a safe environment. The value base of PEPS requires PEs to ensure that they *recognise and work to prevent unjustifiable discrimination and disadvantage in all aspects of the assessment process and counter any unjustifiable discrimination in ways that are appropriate to their situation and role* (Value 6). In practical terms, this includes finding out about any support systems accessible to students within your workplace or wider agency. This may include groups for black workers, LGBT support groups, anti-discrimination and anti-bullying policies and so on. You may usefully agree with other PEs to arrange peer supervision groups – a model successfully followed in a number of areas – especially by agencies with several bases taking several students at one time, perhaps with a wide geographical spread.

Education

All professional frameworks require social workers to maintain up-to-date knowledge and skills relating to their practice area. The PEPS further require PEs to *teach the learner using contemporary social work models, methods and theories relevant to the work, powers and duties, and policy and procedures of the agency, demonstrating the ability for critical reflection* (Domain B:1). It is therefore essential for you to ensure that you have access to all the most recent knowledge in your practice area and the resources and materials necessary to teach your student.

Management

The PE has responsibility for ensuring a placement follows the structure and procedures required by the university. Later in this chapter we will look at how you facilitate the student's involvement in this. However, you will inevitably be responsible for identification and allocation of work (perhaps in conjunction with a team manager) and for ensuring acceptable standards of practice are maintained, above all with regard to safety of service users. This brings us to the question of accountability. You need to be very clear as to the limits of the student's accountability – some tasks are simply not possible for a student and in most teams the PE retains accountability for the practice of the student. However, PEs should also ensure that allocation of certain work to students is not inadvertently avoided simply because they are a student – you should be aware of your assumptions in this area (Values Statement 1, PEPS). It is therefore helpful before the placement to make sure that you have mechanisms in place to monitor and agree issues of accountability, autonomy and discretion – whether through supervision with your own manager, or proof-reading and screening processes which may involve other members of the team.

Preparation of workplace, colleagues and service users/carers

Your personal preparation is only one of the key aspects of preparation for a student. Another is to prepare colleagues and the wider team. It is important to be clear that you are not alone in being responsible for the student. You are there to facilitate their learning – in the team setting. You should involve your colleagues and encourage them to contribute as much as possible – students need access to a skill mix, and, where possible, to a multi-disciplinary environment. You should talk to your colleagues beforehand, with a view to involving them in teaching sessions, shadowing opportunities, joint working, even assessment opportunities. Research into how organisations can effectively support practice learning emphasises the significance of a formal practice learning strategy, embedding practice learning into team practices and supporting PEs with CPD strategies (Doel 2006). However as Williams and Rutter (2010) discuss, you cannot naively assume all members of a team will feel positively towards a student. Previous negative experiences may influence reception of another student; current issues within workplaces and organisations may lead to anxiety and reluctance to host a student placement. In social work agencies generally practitioners are reporting increased stress and workloads – quite separately from the changes being effected by the introduction of the new professional frameworks. Indeed, as a PE you may feel anxious about supervising and assessing a student under a new framework with which you are not familiar.

Crucial to recent developments in social work education have been the explicit calls to involve service users and carers in a meaningful fashion. A review of the participation of service users and carers in social work education (Wallcraft *et al.*, 2012) found that although many universities had well-established partnerships with service users and carers, there was little evidence of the impact of this on students' practice. It is imperative that we reconsider our approach to ensure that placements maximise opportunities for students to learn alongside service users and their carers. Universities require that service user/carer perspective is embedded within the evidence your student presents in their portfolio and which you draw upon for your assessment. There are numerous existing models of questionnaires developed by service user-led groups, agencies and universities which elicit service user/carer perspectives on their contact with students. However, there may well be more creative ways in which you can facilitate the involvement of service users/carers in both the teaching and assessing of students on placement. If you have a local service user-led group you could approach them or ask your university practice learning co-ordinator for ideas. There are national service user groups such as Shaping our Lives (www.shapingourlives.org.uk) which has been involved since the early 2000s in developing social work degree programmes (see the section 'Taking it further' at the end of this chapter for an additional helpful reference).

The GSCC Code of Practice (GSCC, 2002) was based upon a statement of expectations which was developed directly from consultation with service users and carers. This explicit and visible influence should not be lost. The requirement for universities to work with service users/carers in assessing students' readiness for direct practice (discussed above) is but one way of embedding their perspective in social work education from the outset.

As the placement moves nearer it may be helpful to begin to formulate a *practice learning plan*. This will help you specifically analyse the learning requirements and objectives of the student in the light of the learning opportunities you plan to make available. The plan will be added to and informed by your first meeting and subsequent knowledge of the student. Chapter 4 takes this further with a discussion of a Practice Learning Curriculum.

Moving from general preparation to preparation for working with a particular individual

You will receive details of a prospective student from your agency practice learning co-ordinator, or direct from a university. This is variously called the student placement request form, or student profile. This is the point at which you will begin to form an assessment of the particular student's needs. You will typically be given the student's contact details, level of study, and a synopsis of their previous experience and qualifications. You should also be informed of any additional needs the student may have relating to disability, health needs or caring responsibilities, as well as learning needs related to the placement itself. In the spirit of the PCF it is likely that the university will have encouraged or required the student to maintain a personal and professional development portfolio. This should help to inform progress through placements, and subsequently form the foundation of their first year in practice and ASYE.

You are thus likely to hold a lot of information about the student before you meet, and while that can inform the development of your practice learning plan, aspects of the PEPS values statements become particularly significant at this point. You are required to respect the individual needs and strengths of a student, and assess them in a non-discriminatory manner (Values 3–6). Nevertheless, your assessment should be fair and in line with professional standards (see Chapter 6).

There may be circumstances described on the placement request form that mean you have to prepare or adapt the workplace or make enquiries as to flexibility of working patterns. You need to be sure about your workplace's attitude to flexible working, along with the university requirement. Where necessary, consult with your agency or university practice learning co-ordinators. A useful resource is the PEdS Project (University of Hull, 2005) (see Wray *et al.*, 2005), which looks closely at the provision of reasonable adjustments, where relevant.

The pre-placement meeting

We use this term here to describe the first meeting between student and PE. While often described as the informal meeting, in many ways this is the most crucial point of the placement as it sets the scene for the coming months.

The pre-placement meeting should take place before any final decision is taken as to whether the placement can proceed. Its purpose is for the student and PE to identify the needs, concerns and interests of the student, and to agree whether suitable learning opportunities are available for the student to demonstrate their capability. Issues of disability or other identified specific needs should be clearly discussed. Some universities have produced a proforma for the pre-placement meeting to promote discussion and to ensure that issues and agreements are taken forward and shared with the university tutor at the Practice Learning Agreement Meeting.

On occasion the pre-placement meeting will end with an agreement that the placement cannot proceed. This may be for practical reasons, or sometimes relate to the presentation of the student or specific needs that cannot be met. If this occurs it is essential that this is discussed and clear feedback given to the student and relevant practice learning co-ordinator.

The arrival of the student

The second part of this chapter will look at four themes that concern themselves with placement planning when the student has arrived; the learning environment, induction, involving the learner and effective working relationships. As an introduction to these themes, the reader is encouraged to reflect on these additional critical questions which seek to challenge some common assumptions:

Critical **questions**

- » In what way can the agency promote a learning environment and view itself as a 'team around the student'?

- » How can I encourage the student to be an active participant in the planning process?

» How can we ensure induction is part of the process curriculum, and not merely an introduction?

The learning environment

The environment in which the student learns is one of the singularly most important elements of the placement as it may fundamentally affect the success or otherwise of the learning experience and reflect the essence of the culture towards learning in the organisation. Of course, the description 'environment' does not relate solely to the physical aspects, although these are important – but equally to the culture within the team and organisation. Does the organisation essentially strive for technical competence or does it promote critical and reflective thinkers so that research, creativity and developmental practice are valued and encouraged – supported by a sympathetic infrastructure and ethos? As PEs we have a responsibility to help students make connections between the learning environment and service delivery. It is hard sometimes for students to understand that while their needs as learners are important, it is the needs of the people who use the services that are paramount. An organisational culture that values people and is committed to enhancing their well-being and development, promotes learning. As students are introduced to the norms and values of the organisation, they will inevitably make connections between those that promote well-being and put the needs of the service users first, and how the organisation nurtures its own staff. The learning organisation may well mirror its treatment of service users and staff. This is an issue for students, practitioners, PEs, their host agency and, of course, the profession as a whole. Since 2012 agencies have been invited to apply for a quality badge known as 'endorsement' from TCSW and have their efforts in providing and promoting learning encouraged and validated.

A student's idea of what makes for a good learning environment is likely to differ between individuals and what is significant to them. However, the quality of the relationship with the PE is a key factor for success and while the organisation as a whole is important, this supervisory relationship is a key sphere of influence for the PE in creating a positive learning environment. According to Handy (1991) organisations need the *E factor* – excitement, enthusiasm, effervescence and energy. Placements are to be enjoyed, as well as being assessed-learning experiences, and it is important to foster these qualities in students. But the enjoyment of the student is not the only focus; PEs commonly make the point that they have learned just as much *from* the student as they have delivered *to* the student.

A similar synchronicity applies in other ways. To be good enablers we also need to be committed learners, and by so doing we retain a knowledge and understanding of what it is like to be a learner at the different stages of our profession (Beverley and Worsley, 2007). This is explored further in Chapter 9. However, there are some challenges in establishing a suitable climate where learners feel comfortable enough that they are willing to be challenged about their assumptions – and also confident enough to explore new ways of thinking. How free is your student to make mistakes?

Professional **development prompt**

What features identify your team as a positive learning environment? Create a list and order them in terms of significance. Ask a colleague to do the same – do you share a similar view?

While the physical environment may contribute to the overall atmosphere, the quality of the relationships within the team usually supersede the physical environment's impact. Are there any race, disability or gender issues? How is difference managed? What is the composition of the team and how might that impact on the student? You may wish to consider how problems are dealt with in your team.

Thinking more specifically of your student you will need to examine and reflect upon the mechanisms for allocating appropriate work to the student and what type of work is available. Do your colleagues understand the requirements of social work training and the frameworks and model of assessment? You may need to brief your team and/ or manager or indeed, identify some training needs of your own that you will need to address. Are colleagues with specialist skills or knowledge prepared to spend time with the student? Evidently a learning environment is not just for students but will encompass the needs of all staff by promoting the value of learning and professional development for all.

Professional **development prompt**

Consider how you might influence and promote a learning culture in your team/organisation in one or more of the following ways.

» Form a study group.

» Read, think and talk about new ideas.

» Attend training and conferences.

» Start a support group for PEs and mentors.

» Be willing to share power with your student.

It may be that you need to model in order to encourage colleagues. As a member of a team who may not have line manager responsibility for staff, is there any way you are able to foster a climate of learning and continuous professional development within your team/organisation? It is interesting to note that as the role of the PE becomes embedded in the profession through the deployment of the PCF, PEs will more and more be seen to have a leadership role in encouraging the concept of a learning organisation. While the PE is expected to be at least at the level of an experienced social worker, the ability to move through the capabilities as experience and knowledge develop provide for a more defined career structure and sphere of influence in Practice Education.

Induction – the learning starts here

Students often talk about – and think of – induction as a set period of time – a planned programme approach (Ford and Jones, 1987). However, it is usually most helpful to consider induction as taking place over a less defined period of time and to constitute an experience acquired as the student assumes their role in the agency. In planning induction, it is important to take account of the student's individual needs, their confidence and interests – information best obtained before the placement begins. Good placement planning and a thorough induction will help the student to feel welcome, to become familiar with the requirements of their role, and to understand the agency's structure and policies. Induction, however, should not be a random series of events; it is a method of learning about the organisation, its work, and partner agencies, as well as its culture and unwritten rules. Induction needs to be a purposeful activity and linked to intended outcomes. Incidentally, the author recalls as a student on the first day of placement refusing the proffered cup of milky coffee at 11am and tea at 3pm. It was a team ritual I did not know about – and helping your student 'fit in' means unpacking for them the rituals and routines of office life. Pay attention to the softer areas of induction, as well as the policies to read and the people to see.

When the student starts, ensure that you are around. Being present is a mark of respect and of placing the student's experience above the day-to-day demands of workload pressures on that special day. Involve the student; it is important to negotiate elements of the induction package – this is a measure of respect for their experience and their views as a learner about what they would like to engage with in a period of induction. It is also an empowering approach. Is the student happy with its pace and content?

Can the student arrange some visits to key agencies themselves, and so on? Some visits are better later in the placement when the student is more familiar with the work of the agency. Evans (1999) identifies three main principles for inducting students:

1. involving the student in the whole process;

2. involving other people in the programme, including service users;

3 allowing students time to be comfortable in their immediate work base before involving them with other agencies/teams and their staff associated with the work base.

This latter is important. Some students judge the value of their induction on how many external agency visits have been arranged for them without considering the overall learning objectives, so you may need to reassure them of the possibilities of 'induction' over a broader arc of the placement – as well as the need to prioritise certain learning opportunities at different times: an important professional skill.

Exercise

Construct an induction programme for a student. Begin by compiling a list of activities in sections, eg internal to the organisation, external, etc. Try to prioritise.

» What does the student need to know about (key agency policies/ procedures)?

» Who does the student need to meet (including other agencies)?

Activity: role play

Ask one of your colleagues to role play an incoming student, with you in the role of PE. You are seeing the student for the first supervision session – discuss the induction package and complete a supervision agreement with them (covering what supervision will be used for; expectations on both sides; who will record the minutes, etc.).

A useful starting point for considering what needs to be included in an induction package is provided by Evans (1999) who suggests that the student should gradually *proceed outwards* from the base – ie the student meeting key people in the team; shadowing colleagues, etc. and familiarising themselves with the team function and processes and then meeting key partner agencies 'outside' the base. Seeking feedback on induction, and reflecting on the experiences, is an important activity for students as it helps you as a PE evaluate the programme you have provided, and provides the student with an opportunity to begin to think about their own CPD record.

Involving the student

We will now look at how students can actively participate in learning, and the mechanisms by which this can be facilitated, focusing particularly on the foundation building blocks of the Learning Agreement – and the structure and content of the first supervision session. These two events are crucial in establishing a positive learning environment. Part of being a capable professional is having the ability to be an independent and self-motivated learner (Barnett and Coate, 2005) and it is important that learners are able to manage their learning as part of their professional role. Students should be encouraged to:

» self-identify their learning needs although this may only be a partial picture as PEs will know how individual learning needs will link with the PCF (and, to a lesser extent, the SOPS);

» organise some learning objectives;

» be involved in setting up and/or participating in induction;

» identify and transfer existing skills and knowledge.

Taking responsibility for one's own learning can improve learning outcomes and is a skill that is important for professional development, reflective practice and outcomes for service users. Of course this will be different for individual students and will depend on ability, confidence and the extent to which the student can utilise her/his transferable skills. The Learning Agreement can enshrine important first principles related to responsibility for learning.

The Learning Agreement

This is a written document discussed and agreed at a meeting between the student, PE and university tutor, usually before the placement begins or in the first two weeks of the placement start date.

A Learning Agreement is a written agreement between a student and their PE about the particular knowledge, skills and attitudes the student will develop. It allows the student to make the best of available learning opportunities during practice place-ments. It also enables the student to identify and focus upon individual learning needs and begin to focus on the assessment frameworks.

The PE's role and responsibilities in relation to Learning Agreements

The PE plays a key role in the creation of a positive, challenging, learning environment that enables students to develop both professional capability and professional iden-tity. This entails:

> » providing an orientation to the practice placement, area of work and range of potential opportunities for learning;

> » engaging in discussions to help analyse learning needs, identifying learning opportunities and matching these to desired learning outcomes;

> » collaboration with the learner to devise personal and professional goals that are both realistic and relevant to the practice placement;

> » acting as a facilitator and resource towards achieving the goals of the Learning Agreement;

> » assistance in evaluating success in the process of achieving the goals in the Learning Agreement.

Neil Thompson (2006b) discusses the need to set parameters and clarify expecta-tions. He advises that the document is not a *rigid blueprint* and can be adapted to the changes in the placement environment and in the pace of the learner. This is perhaps an ideal way in which to involve the student in planning their own learn-ing on the programme. It is, however, important to help students to differentiate between their learning needs and the opportunities available on placement as they are not necessarily the same thing. For example, there may be a gap between the student who wants to learn about safeguarding issues, and the typical remit of the agency. While indirect learning opportunities (reading, research, visits, etc.) can always be found, they may not be what the student expects – this may need to be clarified. There will have been some initial identification of learning needs from the student's profile, their informal visit to the agency and of course in the Learning Agreement meeting. Pay close attention to these agendas to avoid confusion and disappointment.

Students will vary in confidence and experience in being able to understand what role they will have in the placement, how the learning opportunities will equip them for practice, and translating this into learning needs. For example, a student's construction of supervision – what to expect, what will be discussed, and so forth – might be based on quite different experiences to your own. Like service users and carers, students are not 'helpless' and should be able to recognise their own needs and take responsibility, but you will have a role in helping explore and focus these needs especially in the early days of placement.

The Learning Agreement meeting provides an opportunity for students to articulate their learning needs beyond the desire to 'learn everything' or remain vague by referring to generic skills such as 'communicating with service users'. The tutor may play a pivotal role here by preparing the student for this meeting. It is a reasonable expectation that students arrive at placement with a working knowledge of the broad expectations and roles within a placement setting. As this meeting is the base line from which the placement progresses it is important that its product – the Learning Agreement – is seen as a working document and that reference will be made to it from time to time to ensure that the work is proceeding as planned. All too often the Learning Agreement is completed and put away only to resurface if problems arise, or maybe when included in the placement portfolio. It is important to model good practice and use the agreement as a working document in much the same way as students should use their planning and assessment documents within their own caseload. The PE's skill is in engaging in the triad of student, PE and tutor to explore, exchange and negotiate. It is a professional discussion and perhaps one of the first learning opportunities for the student to engage in inter-professional negotiation.

First supervision session

With the Learning Agreement in place, there is usually only a short time before the initial supervision session. Both PE and student may be somewhat apprehensive about this event and, of course, the PE carries the primary responsibility for making this session work well.

Supervision is the central focus of Chapter 5, but it is good practice to introduce the concept of supervision in induction as it emphasises its importance and also provides the student with the opportunity to understand its purposes, particularly around teaching and assessment.

Supervision Agreement

It is good practice to negotiate a Supervision Agreement with the student. This is not the same as a Learning Agreement. The Learning Agreement made at the beginning of the placement may facilitate this process but is primarily devised by the educational programme and sets broad parameters. The concept of the Supervision Agreement helps to facilitate communication between PE and student, making for a well thought-out practice learning experience and thereby a higher quality supervised professional experience.

Professional **development prompt**

Here are some ideas about what a Supervision Agreement might contain. Reflect on each and think how you might discuss these with a student. Are there more you might add?

» Time and place of supervision.

» Roles and expectations.

» Dealing with interruptions.

» Acknowledgement and management of power issues.

» Confidentiality and its limits.

» Recording supervision notes.

Effective working relationships

Getting to know the student is an important task. Just as the casework relationship is seen as central to good practice in social work, the relationship between student and PE can be seen as central to good teaching practice – and team colleagues also have an important role to play. Involving students in planning and identifying objectives helps to establish and maintain the relationship between educator and learner, but there are other networks that need to be considered. Attention needs to be paid to the nexus between the student, tutor and yourself. The tutor and the HEI they represent are a central concern for the student and placement meetings; university recall days and course documentation are all expressions of areas where effective relationships and understandings are important. Ford and Jones (1987), helpfully unpack the key principles involved in this complex three way – or 'tripartite' – relationship. They argue that openness and honesty is essential between tutor and PE, based on a sufficient degree of confidence and trust in respective abilities. It is important that both PE and tutor also demonstrate genuine care and respect for the student. Finally, it is important that 'openness' is exhibited in meetings – even in difficult arenas. It also has to be understood, though, that at times any pair (PE and student, tutor and student, PE and tutor), has to be able to discuss problems freely in the absence of the third party (Ford and Jones 1987). In this way, effective working relationships will support both PE and student in progressing through a placement.

Conclusion

This chapter has looked closely at the challenges faced by PEs before the placement begins and in its early days. PEs need to think carefully how their agency and workplace appear to the 'outsider' and how they can work towards creating a strong learning culture in their organisation – this can sometimes be difficult. Placement planning begins before the student arrives; it involves the team and an awareness of the work, culture and norms of behaviour. The arrival of the student is signified by a planned induction period, with placement meetings with the tutor helping to set up a clear Learning Agreement and a separate Supervision Agreement. These are the building blocks for an effective placement.

What does the research say?

While individual PEs and teams are central to the provision of an effective learning experience for students, the wider organisation and the learning environment are also important.

The wider organisation

There has been some research into how agencies and Local Authorities can more effectively organise practice learning and how staff can be supported in delivering practice learning opportunities.

The Practice Learning Taskforce (PLTF) was a Department of Health-funded initiative that ran from January 2003 to March 2006, whose purpose was to increase the quantity and diversity of practice learning opportunities and improve the quality of placements. The PLTF published research and the findings of its work in the *Capturing the Learning* series of publications (Practice Learning Taskforce, 2006). One of the research reports within the series – *Effective practice learning in local authorities (1): Strategies for improvement (2006)* by Professor Mark Doel – offers some useful insights and suggestions into how agencies and Local Authorities can support and nurture placements and those offering them, and develop new opportunities. The report includes a sample of 20 Local Authorities in England, including staff involved in practice learning at different levels. Data collection was via completion of questionnaires, attendance at workshops, and a focus group.

Key messages highlighted in the research include:

» the need for organisational commitment to practice learning, including identified *practice learning champions* within Local Authorities – at the senior management level and also *in the ranks* (Doel, 2006, p. 15);

» the significance of a formal practice learning strategy, involving strategic planning for practice learning provision and development. Suggestions included practice learning as a target of team performance and practice learning included in job descriptions;

» embedding practice learning and recognising the links with recruitment and retention; encouraging teams to take on students and provide a positive experience as a way of enhancing recruitment to the authority, and retaining current staff;

» recognising the importance of practice learning and placements as part of staff CPD; offering support, incentives, training and workload relief to PEs and valuing the role they fulfil;

» the importance of a team approach to practice learning and development of a learning culture characterised by a shared commitment and responsibility for practice learning across teams.

The learning environment

To enable effective learning PEs have to ensure that the learning environment is appropriate and safe for a student. There are many aspects that contribute to an appropriate learning environment – PE experience, motivation and skills; the student's previous experiences, skills and approach to learning; the 'atmosphere' in the team and, as noted above, the support offered to practice learning within the wider setting.

One of the critical factors that impacts on the learning environment is the relationship between the PE and the student. This is supported by research in the UK and elsewhere (Fernandez, 1998; Parker, 2010a Wilson *et al.* 2009). Research carried out by Michelle Lefevre (2005) outlines the significance of this relationship.

The sample included 44 social work students in a UK university who had successfully completed either one or two placements, involving 77 placement experiences overall. Data collection was via a survey and completed written questionnaires.

Key messages highlighted in the research include:

- » 90 per cent of the students felt their relationship with their PE had an impact on their learning and development;

- » students valued PEs who were 'supportive' (a term used by almost half of student respondents); with whom they could build relationships of trust and who were constructive, 'available' and collaborative in their way of working;

- » students valued PEs who organised the placement well and provided a well-structured placement and who were open and transparent about the assessment process;

- » students also appreciated PEs who demonstrated skills, knowledge and values both in social work and in their role as PEs. Students valued PEs who were skilled in identifying theory and linking it to practice;

- » an appropriately supportive environment helped students accept and use critical feedback as an aid to developing their practice.

Taking it further

Thompson, N., Osada, M. and Anderson, B. (1994) *Practice Teaching in Social Work*, Birmingham: PEPAR.

Evans, D. (1999*) Practice Learning in the Caring Professions*, Hampshire: Ashgate.

These present a comprehensive approach to practice learning, and the principles they espouse are still relevant today.

Williams, S. and Rutter, L. (2013, 2nd ed.) *The Practice Educators Handbook*, Exeter: Learning Matters.

A more recent text which has been updated to refer to the new professional frameworks and explores how the PEPS (2013b) domains can be methodically applied to PE practice.

In order to assist in taking a methodical and comprehensive approach to planning the placement, the following books are recommended. They refer to the National Occupational Standards (TOPSS, England 2002a); however, they contain activities and themes which continue to be relevant to work with students.

Maclean, S. and Caffrey, B. (2009) *Developing a Practice Curriculum*, Rugeley: Kirwin Maclean Associates Ltd.

Maclean, S. and Lloyd, I. (2013 2nd Edition) *Developing Quality Practice Learning in Social Work: A Straightforward Guide for Practice Teachers and Supervisors*, Rugeley: Kirwin Maclean Associates Ltd.

To continue the theme of student-centred practice, PEs may find it useful to look at books specifically aimed at students beginning practice learning. The following have been recommended by students:

Lomax, R., Jones, K., Leigh, S. and Gay, C. (2010) *Surviving Your Social Work Placement*, Basingstoke: Palgrave Macmillan.

Parker, J. (2010) *Practice Learning in Social Work*. Exeter: Learning Matters.

Edmondson, D. (2013) *Social Work Practice Learning: A student guide*. London: Sage.

Finally, to help PEs and students develop service user/carer-focused practice, the following is recommended:

Social Care Institution for Excellence (2013) *Co-production in social care: what is it and how to do it*. London: SCIE.

The material in this chapter links to the following PEPS domains and values statements for PEs and supervisors:

Learning outcome domains required for Stage 1 and Stage 2 PEs

A:1; B:1; B:2; B:3; B:4; B:5; B:6; B:7; B:8; B:9; C:8; C:9

Additional learning outcome domains required for Stage 2 PEs

D:1; D:6

Values for PEs and supervisors: 1–4

Chapter aims

» To consider the role of the Practice Educator (PE) as an enabler and facilitator of student learning on placement.

» To consider some of the key concepts underpinning student learning including the importance of the learning environment; adult learning; the role of 'experiential' learning and the place of learning needs, motivations and learning styles in understanding learning.

» To consider the planning and the charting of the 'learning journey' of the student and the role of the 'Practice Curriculum' within the placement.

» To examine how the PE can develop their enabling style and teaching strategies that the PE can use.

Critical **questions**

» What can I do to facilitate and promote student learning? How can I use the PCF to help me in my role as an enabler?

» What teaching strategies can I use to 'teach' the student? How can I help the student relate theory to practice?

> » The students learning journey – how will I structure the student's learning and development on placement?
>
> » How will I develop my enabling style? How can I enhance and extend my own learning?

Introduction

TCSW notes that *effective practice placements are the cornerstone of students' learning* ('Overview of new arrangements for practice learning', TCSW, undated, www.tcsw.org.uk/uploadedFiles/TheCollege/_CollegeLibrary/Reform_resources/ Practice-Learning(edref7).pdf). The previous chapter explored some of the necessary requirements to achieve this. The pivotal role of the PE in ensuring effective practice placements – as educators of social work students and as enablers and facilitators of student learning on placement – is outlined in the PEPS (TCSW, 2013b). The PEPS Domain B in particular, notes the role of the PE in supporting learning and professional development in practice, through awareness of adult learning models, learning needs and the co-ordination of learning opportunities, along with direct teaching.

This chapter will refer briefly to some of the key concepts and ideas underpinning learning – the influences on learning and some of the barriers to learning; the principles of adult learning; the necessity of understanding motivation and learning styles and their use in learning; how learning happens and the role of experiential learning. Many of these key ideas should have been included in the PE training you have undertaken and have also been covered in detail in other texts about practice learning, and particular relevant texts and chapters are noted in the 'Taking it further' section at the end of this chapter. However, the main focus of this chapter will be on the enabling and teaching role of the PE and what they can do to facilitate student learning on placement.

Key concepts underpinning learning

What influences learning?

There are many influences on learning – Thompson (2006b) refers to these influences operating within two contexts – the organisational context of learning, and the social context of learning. The organisational context of learning refers to the influence of factors such as the 'learning culture' of the organisation or team and the learning environment within it. He suggests that learning will be enhanced if there is a positive 'learning culture' within the organisation and/or team. Chapter 3, looking at preparation, planning and induction, invited you to consider the learning environment and to look at your team 'from the outside' and consider how it might be experienced by a student. As the PE you can influence and promote a positive learning environment in a number of ways – by promoting and seeking the active involvement of others in the student's learning; through modelling continuing learning and a commitment to lifelong learning and by ensuring that you treat the relationship between you and the student as a true *learning partnership* (Beverley and Worsley, (2007, p. 19). The notion of a learning partnership is also strengthened by an acknowledgement that learning on placement is a shared enterprise – it is not simply for the PE to 'teach' the student and provide the learning opportunities; the student as part of their professional development is expected to take responsibility for managing their learning and to respond to the opportunities given. This is highlighted in the HCPC *Guidance on conduct and ethics for students*, Standard 6 which advises students that they are responsible for their own learning; also, PCF Domain 1 requires that students act on their own learning needs (first placement level indicators) and, at the final level placement, demonstrate a commitment to their continuous learning and development.

The social context of learning (Thompson, 2006b) refers to the influence of factors such as prior experiences of learning – students may have had poor experiences of formal education and come to new experiences lacking in confidence regarding their abilities to learn and progress; this may also be related to structural barriers and issues of class, race or gender. Lack of confidence and self-belief can thus be a barrier to learning but there can also be others – the student's particular circumstances, such as caring responsibilities for example, can have an impact, as can learner anxiety. Such anxiety is common to us all when experiencing new situations and Rogers (1989) reminds us that some tension and anxiety will always be present when real learning is taking place. For a social work student in a time-limited placement, where they are being assessed on their capabilities and values at the same time as working with vulnerable people, their awareness of 'what they don't know' and fear of 'getting it wrong', can be hugely anxiety provoking. Thompson (2006b) suggests in these circumstances the PE and the student need to ensure that issues of anxiety are acknowledged and that while students should not be *nursemaided* (p. 24), the PE should be *calming, reassuring and supportive* (p. 24). In their role as an enabler, the PE is aiming to provide or contribute to an environment that will enhance adult learning processes.

Adult learning

In considering how adults learn, Knowles (1990) also pointed to the importance of the learning environment and the need to involve adult learners in their own learning. He referred to the concept of *andragogy* and discussed common principles about the ways in which adults learn.

> » Adults have pre-existing knowledge and experiences that can be built upon and used.

> » Adults have a motivation to learn; this motivation can sustain learning.

> » Adults are goal oriented and need to place learning in the context of wider goals and achievement of objectives.

> » Adults are motivated by relevancy – learning is enhanced when adults can see the relevancy of a learning activity.

These principles can help PEs understand student learning, but it is still important not to make any assumptions about the student based on these principles. As a PE you will need to get to know your student and find out about their learning needs and uncover their individual motivations. As the previous chapter indicated, many students will come to a placement with a written list of their 'learning needs' and sometimes these can be very broad ('improve my communication skills') or can be a list of 'things I want to do' on placement ('gain experience of report writing'). A deeper and more thoughtful approach – recognising that motivation is a key condition for learning – is one that considers and seeks to unearth motivations for learning, as understanding these motivations can guide and inform the PE's approach. Social work students may come to placement motivated by extrinsic factors; for example, to gain the professional qualification for entry into social work and a new career. However, intrinsic factors and motivations for learning – openness to learning and development; being excited by new ideas and ways of working; seeing the opportunities that the placement offers not just for 'passing' but for challenges and rewards in relation to professional and self-development – are often the impetus both for meaningful learning and sustained motivation within the placement. The expectations within PCF Domain 1 – *Professionalism* – also require that a student demonstrates a commitment to continuous learning and development.

The role of learning styles

It is considered that learners have a preferred learning style – preferences or habits for learning in a certain way. One of the most well-known models of identifying and

characterising learning styles is that offered by Honey and Mumford (1992) who identify four different types of learners: Reflectors, Theorists, Activists and Pragmatists.
Further details of each learning style and indication of the learning strategies and
tasks that may be effective for each is given in Appendix 2. As a PE an awareness of
your own learning style and how you prefer to learn is essential for your role as an
enabler of others – you and the student may not have the same preferences for learning and this may be a challenge for you. Beverley and Worsley (2007) suggest that,
not surprisingly perhaps, many of us 'teach' according to our own preferred learning style. Thus, a social worker/PE with a 'preferred' reflector/theorist style, when
allocated a new service user to work with, may ensure (and relish) some 'preparing,
thinking and theorising' time before any initial contact with the service user. A student with a more activist approach to learning may feel more comfortable 'getting
out there' rather than discussing or considering presenting issues in detail, and the
PE may be surprised and challenged by the student's reluctance to discuss possible
relevant issues before initial contact. Keeping the centrality of the learner/student
in mind, the PE will need to consider how they will match their 'enabling' style with
the student's 'learning style' (Beverley and Worsley, 2007), and ensure that the student has enough information to make initial contact but also making certain that
time is allocated for discussion and reflection after the initial visit. As the PE, this
will involve challenging your own assumptions and comforts about how you learn/
teach, and consideration about how you will provide varied learning experiences for
the student.

The use of learning styles in understanding learning also comes with cautions.
Shardlow and Doel (1996) warn that identifying learning styles can suggest that
learning styles are fixed and unchangeable, when they are not. They can be helpful
to use with students as they can help both student and PE in the learning partnership – they can assist the student in an awareness of their approaches to learning and
identify areas which they need to develop and strengthen and they can help you as the
PE in considering the most effective way to approach or suggest a learning task to the
student.

How learning happens – the role of experiential learning

Jarvis and Gibson (1997) define learning as *the transformation of experience into
knowledge, skills, attitudes, emotions, beliefs, senses* and thus that *all learning begins
with experience* (p. 56). One of the best known illustrations of learning, particularly
workplace learning, is Kolb's experiential learning cycle (1984).

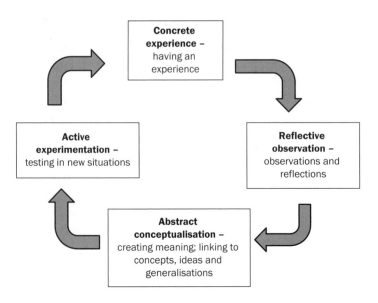

Kolb (1984) thus demonstrates the value of experiential learning, although learning from experience may not be a single or simple process; it may include a number of diverse experiences. However, the importance of this model lies in its assertions that learning is not simply the 'acquisition' of knowledge as a result of experience, but requires reflection and a focus on the essential processes involved. Race (2007) offers another model of learning which includes the issues of motivation and feedback and is more of a 'ripples in a pond' model – where factors overlap with each other – than a circular model.

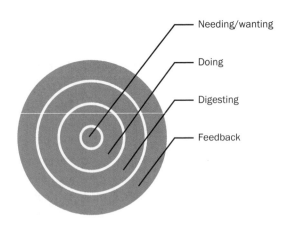

> » Needing/wanting – learners should have motivation, should need/want to do/learn something.

> » Doing – learners must be able to practise, trial and error; applying the learning.

> » Digesting – making sense of what has been done (feeding back into further doing, and digesting, making sense again).

> » Feedback – seeing the results, seeking others' reactions and gaining feedback (coming from various sources and feeding back into digesting, thinking again and doing again ...)

It can be seen how incorporating aspects of doing, reflecting, feedback and digesting into all learning activities and teaching methods on placement will be helpful to students with different learning styles.

Consideration of these key concepts underpinning learning will contribute to PEs' understanding and achievement of PEPS Domains A:1; A:7; B:2, B:3, B:4, B:5 and Values for Practice Educators and supervisors 2, 3, 4 and 5.

Enabling and teaching

This section will consider how the PE can apply their understanding of learning in their work with students on placement and will consider the areas and elements of enabling and learning outlined in the critical questions at the beginning of this chapter.

What is the PE aiming to achieve and how can the PE facilitate and promote student learning?

Integration of practice and theory

The PCF and the expectations regarding the professional development of a capable, knowledgeable and critically reflective holistic practitioner is a helpful place to start when considering what PEs are aiming to achieve when working with social work students on placement. The PCF implicitly incorporates what Barnett and Coate (2005) refer to as the domains of *knowing*, *acting* and *being*, present within all academic and professional subject areas and indicated in the following diagram.

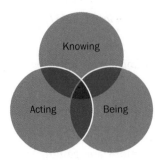

Barnett and Coate (2005) suggest that the size and location of each domain will vary according to subject specialism – for example, those working in or studying the sciences may require an increased 'knowing' and knowledge domain, but a smaller and less integrated 'being' domain. For the professions, however, Barnett and Coate (2005) suggest that the three domains are equally weighted and need to be integrated. Lawson (2013) suggests that in relation to social work, the 'knowing', 'acting' and 'being' domains would include:

> » *Knowing* – includes formal knowledge such as social work theories, practice methods, evidence from research, local knowledge such as resources and procedures. In addition it would include knowledge such as personal experience, practice wisdom and self-and-other awareness.

> » *Being* – encapsulates the practitioner's ability to use the self, including the emotional and social skills necessary to build relationships with service users and colleagues, being aware of the influence of values and attitudes on practice.

> » *Acting* – the 'doing' dimension covers the skills, behaviours, and activities that social workers engage in on an everyday basis.

We can see how these three domains, and in particular their overlapping areas and integration, are helpful when considering student professional development on placement. The PCF, as a professional framework, expects students to engage with their knowledge ('knowing'), to understand and to actively apply it to work with service users ('acting' and using skills in practice) while also displaying a critical awareness of 'being' and understanding the authority embedded in the social work role, the emotional impact of the work, and their use of self in relationships with service users.

Exercise: **knowing, acting and being**

With the student, identify a particular piece or area of work (an assessment; a review of needs, etc.) that the student would undertake as a routine part of a placement within your setting.

In undertaking this piece or area of work, together consider how the student might indicate their understanding and development in light of the PCF domains/level in relation to the model of 'knowing', 'acting' and 'being':

Knowing – you might find PCF Domain 3 and 5 helpful here.

Acting – you might find PCF Domain 6 and 7 helpful here.

Being – you might find PCF Domain 1–4 and 8 helpful here.

As the PE you can encourage the student to consider their practice in this integrated and more holistic fashion, linking it to particular domains of the PCF. Lawson (2013) suggests also that this 'acting', 'being' and 'knowing' model can be used as a diagnostic and formative assessment tool, with students or practitioners, to consider strengths and development needs.

It may also be helpful for PEs to consider Trevithick's (2008; 2012) Knowledge and Skills Framework. Here, Trevithick claims that social work practice is multifaceted, incorporating knowledge from different sources and involving 80 generalist skills and interventions. Social work practice thus involves *knowing what* and *knowing how* (2008, p. 1228) and it is the integration of these two elements that PEs should keep in mind when facilitating the learning of students.

Learning to learn

In further helping PEs understand what they are aiming to achieve when working with social work students, it is also useful to consider the concept of *learning to learn* (Cree, 2005; Gardiner, 1989). This is explained by Cree as *helping students to make learning their own* (p. 63); she suggests that through internalising their learning, the student will be more able to make it 'stick' and also transfer their learning and knowledge to other, new situations. Cree (2005) suggests that *learning to learn* is a skill that can be fostered and supported by others within a facilitative, enabling relationship. Gardiner (1989) refers to this as *meta learning* and describes it thus: *This meta–learning, or learning to learn, can promote transfer of the content and process of learning to contexts other than those in which the original learning arose* (p. 133).

For the PE, this would mean ensuring that a range of learning tasks and opportunities have been provided that have taken account of the underlying principles of adult learning outlined at the beginning of this chapter, but also that the student is given the opportunity for critical reflection, rigorous analysis of their practice and values, and encouraged to consider new and exploratory approaches.

A further helpful metaphor is also provided by Lester (1999). He uses the metaphor of 'mapping' to consider professional development. He suggests that practitioners need to move from being *map readers* (as beginning practitioners), following given and guided paths and ways of working, and develop skills as *map makers*; that is to say becoming inquiring and reflective practitioners who can apply their knowledge in new situations and *uncharted territories* (p. 46).

The PE, in helping to develop the students' abilities in *learning to learn* and moving towards becoming a *map maker* will thus be assisting the student in meeting the requirements of the PCF, particularly at final placement level. Here, the student will be expected to manage complexity, work more autonomously, and be able to demonstrate a commitment to their continuous learning and development.

What teaching strategies can the PE use to facilitate student learning?

It is the experience of the writer that many practitioners attending a Practice Education course often feel worried about the 'teaching' expectations embedded in the PE role and feel that they do not teach nor that they have the skills to do so. One recent participant suggested that this is because PEs are *not teaching in a box*, whereby the PE announces, *Today I am going to teach this ... or today the lesson is...* This suggests that the teaching element is often embedded within other aspects of the PE role and accords with the stress on the facilitative and enabling elements of the PE role we have discussed in this chapter. As noted in the introduction, the PEPS (2013b) acknowledge this enabling role but also note (B:1) that the PE will *directly teach the learner*. Many authors agree that the PE role is multifaceted and that the PE role is indeed wider than just being a teacher (Beverley and Worsley, 2007). Harden and Crosby (2000) suggest that the term 'teacher' involves a number of roles including planner, role model, assessor, information provider, facilitator, supervisor and resource developer. A useful way to begin thinking about the teaching element of the PE role is to first consider what we mean by teaching and how it is carried out.

Approaches to learning

Jarvis and Gibson (1997) describe teaching as the *process of helping others learn* (p. 86) and describe three different approaches and styles of teaching.

1. The *didactic* approach, which assumes that teachers have knowledge to impart and they adopt the style of 'giving out' their knowledge. Students are thus 'empty vessels' to be filled with the teacher's knowledge and are passive recipients of the teacher's knowledge. The teacher is at the centre of this model.

2. The *Socratic* approach, which assumes that students are active thinkers and the teacher's style is thus more questioning, requiring the student to problem-solve and reflect, with an emphasis on 'drawing out' knowledge from the student, rather than simply 'putting in' the teachers knowledge.

3. The *facilitative* approach whereby the teacher ensures the conditions and resources for learning and acts as a resource, guide and adviser to the student in the learning process. The student is at the centre of this model.

It can be seen from these differing approaches that the PE role can incorporate all three approaches – at different times in the placement and for different purposes, and to accommodate differing student learning styles, agency and service user needs or complexity of the task or the information. So, for example, a PE may be using a more 'didactic' approach when providing information and initially explaining a particular policy, a new piece of legislation or a particular underpinning theory to a student. However, this would not be enough to ensure learning and the PE may later use a more Socratic, questioning, approach encouraging the student to critically reflect on the implementation of their learning or the policy or piece of legislation; for example, how it affects service users, what particular skills and knowledge they are using in working with service users within the guidelines of the policy. This will assist with the *learning to learn* and *map maker* ideas mentioned previously – the PE would also need to be using a facilitative approach in the way that they work with the student, and, as the placement progresses, not taking over or overtly directing the student's work but offering guidance and advice regarding the work and the student's learning and offering reading or resources that might help both their work with the service user and their own development.

As Chapter 5 on Supervision suggests, much of the 'teaching' element of the PE role takes place in supervision, alongside an opportunity for reflection and critical analysis of practice and an examination of values. An important part of this is the use of feedback – on practice carried out by the student, on their approach and values, on their overall progress, as well as the explicit feedback that is required after a direct observation (and which is referred to in more detail in Chapter 6 on 'Assessment'). The guidance on feedback offered in this chapter recognises the crucial place that feedback can play in learning, inspiring confidence, and improving student performance and understanding. A key part of this is the way in which the PE manages the feedback process as one strategy that they can use to facilitate and encourage student learning.

Giving feedback – good practice guidance

The following good practice guidance is largely based on suggestions offered by Rogers (1989). She notes that there are two dangers in giving feedback – not giving enough, and giving it in the wrong way. Good practice would suggest the following.

» Give feedback as soon as possible.

» Prepare for the feedback, choose an appropriate time and location and ensure privacy.

» Be clear – it is better to make one or two points which are more likely to be remembered than a long list.

» Think of the language you are using and approach the feedback as a constructive dialogue. Seek the student's views, particularly if you are pointing out a less successful part of the interaction – *I wondered what you felt about that?*

» Give balanced and constructive feedback. This will include praising positives and being supportive, but will also need to include some challenge for the student for continuing learning. The following matrix regarding the balance of support/challenge may be helpful.

High support/low challenge

"that was great"

High support/high challenge

"I really liked the way you encouraged the service user to respond and listened so well...I wonder if she understood some of the terminology you used...?"

Low support/low challenge

"that was okay, bits of it could have been better"

Low support/high challenge

"what did you say that for, at that point? Why didn't you explain it properly?"

» Acknowledge strengths first. Evans (1999) suggests that it is only after a student's strengths have been acknowledged that many students can accept the PE's identification of their weakness. He stresses the importance of encouragement and praise and that *often, it is the practice educator's eagerness to help the student learn how to eradicate weaknesses which reduces their emphasis on strengths which need no alteration* (p. 214).

» Refer to specific behaviours and achievements – eg, *it was good when you said/did …* or, *I didn't find it helpful when you … because…* is better than more general or vague comments such as *that was good* or *I didn't like your general attitude*. Rogers (1989) comments that we learn from our successes *as long as we know why we are being successful* (p. 61).

» Make suggestions and offer alternatives – and whatever feedback you give, make sure the student can act upon it. For example, *You handled the grandmother's presence very well and were skilful in getting her opinion but I felt she had more to say and you cut her short as time was running on … can you think of how you could have dealt with this in another way?* (then, *Perhaps you could have acknowledged that you had another appointment and asked to return to discuss the grandmother's issues another time*).

» Own the feedback – use *I* or *It seemed to me* statements – these are your views and opinions and are based on your thoughts, feelings and values.

» Be aware that giving and receiving feedback is not always easy and can provoke strong feelings of anxiety on both sides – sometimes the PE can 'shy away' from giving challenging feedback or the student can become 'defensive'. Doel *et al.* (1996) suggest treating the feedback as *a valuable source of information rather than as a personal criticism [and] … a way of discovering more about yourself* (p. 78). It follows then, that the PE should also be open to receiving feedback about their practice and take this as a source of information helpful to their developing role as a PE.

A helpful way of remembering these guidelines is via the use of the acronym 'SCORE' – Specific, Clear, Owned, Relevant, Enabling.

Professional **development prompt**

Think about a time when you have received feedback about an aspect of your practice.

Consider what made the feedback helpful or unhelpful?

Did the feedback offer you high support and high challenge? If not, how could the feedback to you have been improved?

Some teaching and facilitating strategies

As has been noted, there are direct and indirect methods of teaching and facilitating student learning on placement. The following is a list of some teaching and enabling strategies that you can use during the placement.

» Direct observation of the student's practice – including feedback and discussion of learning from the observation (see Chapter 6 on Assessment).

» Discussion in supervision – including questioning, probing, prompting reflection (see Chapter 5 on Supervision).

» Role play/rehearsal of a specific task or skill.

» Shadowing – the student observing other practitioners; you (informally) observing the student.

» Joint working – with other colleagues or you.

» Observational visits.

» Guided /suggested reading.

» Setting a specific research task regarding an area of practice/theoretical knowledge.

» Setting a specific written piece of work to aid student theoretical understanding, and as the basis for further discussion.

» Reading, discussing student portfolio written pieces of work or critical reflections.

» Reading, discussing student case recording, assessments, and any 'work related' products.

» Project work – such as developing an agency resource pack; working with a particular group of service users, etc.

» Presentation to the team or colleagues.

» Use of the student's reflective log/accounts and discussions arising from it.

» Discussing case studies or using pre-prepared material with the student.

» Direct teaching – the PE teaching the student about a particular policy, theme or topic.

» Group supervision.

Helping students to use theory in practice

Oko (2008), quoting Susser (1968), states:

'to practise without theory is to sail an unchartered sea. Theory without practice is not to set sail at all.' She further describes theory as 'a theory represents therefore an explanatory framework which attempts to help us make sense of the phenomenon in question – in this case the context of social work. These explanations provide us with an opportunity to hypothesise or make a judgement about what is going on. In other words these ideas and assumptions, when acknowledged, provide us with explanations that can aid our understanding of what the matter is – that is they help us answer the question of what is going on, what can be done and why. Theories essentially *help us structure and organise our thinking and are central to helping us make sense of our practice and what we do.'*

(Oko, 2008, p. 6)

At some point in the placement the student, or you as the PE, will raise the issue of relating theory to practice. Many students will be able to explain what a particular theory is but may be unable to relate this directly to the work they are doing. Others will be able to make the links in retrospect but what PEs should be aiming for is the ability to use theory to inform and understand practice and then to intervene. Many social workers and PEs feel almost as worried as students when it comes to considering 'theory and practice', as often their underpinning knowledge and use of theories has been incorporated into their day-to-day 'practice wisdom' and they are not required to articulate the theory/method or approach underpinning their practice in the same way that students are expected to. The PE's role is to help students put their own knowledge, skills and values into effective practice and to demonstrate their 'working out' – to consider how and why a particular theory, method, model or approach has been used; to justify its use and relevance; and to evaluate how effective it has been.

Lord Laming, in the Victoria Climbié inquiry (2003) suggested social workers needed to practise *respectful uncertainty*, applying critical evaluation and questioning to any information they received and maintaining an open mind. This is more likely to be achieved if an understanding and use of theory is embedded in practice at an early stage, if student social workers understand why and how they are intervening in a particular way and what is underpinning their practice.

Further, some of the PCF domains – Domains 4–7 – specifically demand that the student demonstrate they can apply their understanding of relevant knowledge, theory and models to their practice. The PE role is thus to help the student draw this understanding from their practice, helping them to name and apply examples of theory and models informing their practice and their interventions. There are different ways that the PE can help the student do this, some of which are mentioned below.

> » Using 'reflective questions' during supervision, helping the student to explore, clarify and name particular theories or models underpinning their practice. This is considered in more detail in Chapter 5 on Supervision. Adams and Sheard (2013) also suggest the following.
>
> > » Ask the student to talk through a piece of practice in simple terms, first.

» Did they have a hypothesis beforehand about what might be happening? What did they base this on? Discussion can be around the assumptions that the student might be working with.

» Can they tell you why we need theory and what is the point of it?

» Can they explain the theories that they feel are relevant and why?

» Set them a task to find out about a particular theory by the next supervision session.

» The use of the 'knowledge, values, skills, theories' grid for unpicking underpinning elements of practice. The student can either complete this grid on their own, in preparation for discussion in supervision, or it can be used during supervision with the PE and student considering it together in relation to a particular piece of work or intervention. The use of this grid can also help students when preparing written, practice-related case studies for inclusion in their portfolio, if required.

Knowledge	Theories
Values	Skills

» The use of a particular, visual framework for helping the student identify the theories they are using to inform their practice. An example of this is the Theory Circle (Collingwood, 2005; Collingwood *et al.*, 2008).

The Theory Circle

This is a three-stage process that is used with the student as follows.

Stage 1

Prepare the service user profile 'KIT'. Begin by drawing a stick person and then begin to make a very basic profile (using keywords) which identifies the service user. You may wish to include the following: age, gender, race, culture, history, family, friends, likes, dislikes, life events, significant other agency connections, wants, etc. The profile can be drawn up by the student with the service user or used simply as an exercise in itself.

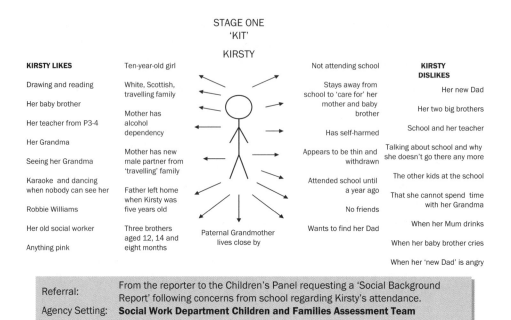

STAGE ONE
'KIT'

KIRSTY

KIRSTY LIKES

Drawing and reading

Her baby brother

Her teacher from P3-4

Her Grandma

Seeing her Grandma

Karaoke and dancing
when nobody can see her

Robbie Williams

Her old social worker

Anything pink

Ten-year-old girl

White, Scottish,
travelling family

Mother has
alcohol
dependency

Mother has new
male partner from
'travelling' family

Father left home
when Kirsty was
five years old

Three brothers
aged 12, 14 and
eight months

Paternal Grandmother
lives close by

Not attending school

Stays away from
school to 'care for' her
mother and baby
brother

Has self-harmed

Appears to be thin and
withdrawn

Attended school until
a year ago

No friends

Wants to find her Dad

**KIRSTY
DISLIKES**

Her new Dad

Her two big brothers

School and her teacher

Talking about school and why
she doesn't go there any more

The other kids at the school

That she cannot spend time
with her Grandma

When her Mum drinks

When her baby brother cries

When her 'new Dad' is angry

Referral: From the reporter to the Children's Panel requesting a 'Social Background
Report' following concerns from school regarding Kirsty's attendance.
Agency Setting: **Social Work Department Children and Families Assessment Team**

Stage 2

Putting Kirsty at the centre the student then surrounds her with the theories that have
informed practice.

STAGE TWO THE THEORY CIRCLE

Theory to inform

Theory to intervene

Attachment and Loss

Human Development

Risk and Resilience

Systems

Mental Health

Self Harm

Travelling families

KIRSTY

Person-centred

Play/work

Behavioural

Life skills

Life story

Geneogram

Stage 3

Finally the student considers what else has informed practice.

STAGE THREE
KNOWLEDGE, SKILLS AND VALUES

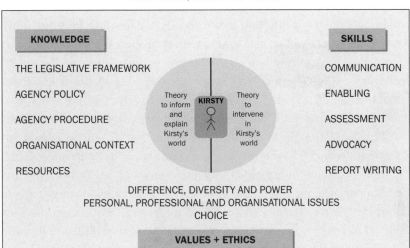

© Collingwood, P, Emond, R and Woodward, R (2008) The Theory Circle: A tool for learning and for practice. *Social Work Education*, 27(1): 70–83

Ensuring an anti-oppressive and strengths-based approach

The importance of the social context of learning and the influence of previous experiences and some of the structural barriers to learning was discussed earlier. Adopting a strengths-based approach to supporting student learning is one way of maintaining an anti-oppressive approach. One model that may be helpful for PEs is the MANDELA model (Tedam, 2012). This was developed by Tedam (2012) in response to the particular issues faced by students of Black African heritage studying on social work courses at her university, where such students were more likely to fail practice placements than white students. This pattern is duplicated in other universities, where Black African students or other black or Asian students are overly represented in failed or terminated placements.

Tedam (2012) asserts that that the MANDELA model can be used by PEs and students to understand and appreciate the differences and similarities of life experience that a student brings to the placement and that *it models best practice in that it provides an open, honest and reflective forum in which discussions about experiences, needs and differences can be examined, respected and understood* (p. 68).

The MANDELA model

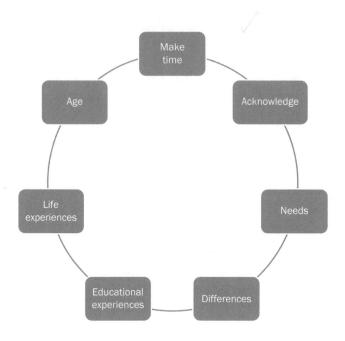

The MANDELA model explained.

Make time
Acknowledge
Needs
Differences
Educational experiences
Life experiences
Age

Make time

> » Do not fast-track the student into difficulty or failing; ensure the student has sufficient time to understand context and nature of the work; make time for supervision at the pace of the student.

Acknowledge **N**eeds

> » Specify any particular needs – these may be English language proficiency skills, general communication skills, written skills, report writing needs; consider how to address these needs and consider from the student's perspective.

Difference

> » After consideration of needs, issues of difference and similarity can be explored. These issues may not only be about ethnic or cultural similarities or differences, there may be issues of gender; consider from the student's perspective.

Educational experience

> » Discuss preferred learning style and comfort with written skills for different purposes and spoken English; discuss educational experiences and previous ways of learning and teaching experienced.

Life experiences

> » Recognise the importance of life experience and what the student brings; explore this area but be cautious as this may be a sensitive area.

Age

> » Within African contexts, age/generation is an important variable in understanding relationships and interactions; age/generational issues may be important with other students.

The MANDELA model was originally developed as a tool to help PEs consider issues relating to a particular group of students, encouraging the exploration of differences and the questioning of assumptions. However, as an example of a strengths-based approach that is helpful in supporting anti-oppressive practice, it is offered here as a model that is suitable for all PEs engaging and encouraging the learning of all students.

Structuring the student's learning journey

As we have discussed so far, the student's 'learning journey' on placement can be affected by a number of issues, which can include; the prior knowledge, skills and experience they bring with them to the placement and how it is valued; their confidence and insight; the relationship with the PE; the team/learning environment; their preferred learning style; the provision of suitable learning opportunities and activities; and the opportunity to reflect, digest and discuss their work and learning. Further, as with most of us facing new circumstances or a new setting or learning a new skill, students can lack confidence or feel 'deskilled' at the start of their placement. This is illustrated in the following 'unconscious/conscious competence' model, taken from www.changingminds.org/explanations/learning/consciousness_competence.htm

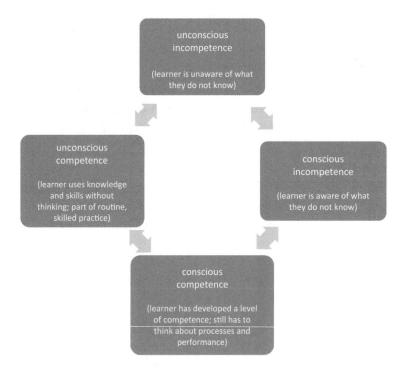

It is important to remember that students (and social workers or PEs) can feel consciously competent (*I am good at …*) some things or aspects of the placement, while feeling consciously incompetent at others (*I am not confident about …*; *I have to think when I am doing … step by step …*). The role of the PE is to acknowledge the 'learning journey' of the student and help them move to 'conscious competence' (in line with the relevant level requirements of the PCF) in as many areas of the work and learning/activities within the placement as possible. This can mean:

» at the *unconscious incompetence* stage the PE will need to focus on helping the student become aware of and acknowledge their learning needs and areas for development;

» at the *conscious incompetence* stage the PE will need to ensure they break down activities and learning into manageable segments; that they source varied and suitable learning opportunities and discuss the student's learning and reflection on their learning in supervision. The PE needs to be reassuring and supportive at this stage, helping the student define, develop and refine their skills, knowledge and understanding;

» at the *conscious competence* stage the PE ensures that good practice and the student's developing confidence and learning are reinforced through regular feedback. There will need to be a focus on continuing areas for development and a discussion with the student about how they might refine their skills, knowledge and understanding;

» at the *unconscious competence* stage the PE will help the student focus on unpacking their knowledge and learning, in order to enable them 'to show their working out', both as a method of confirming areas of strength and also to examine areas for further development. This stage is important in acknowledging that, as the PCF indicates, learning for professional development is rarely completed. The PCF is a developmental framework that requires not only that student social workers need to recognise their learning and training achievements and needs, but so do other practitioners at different levels. Further, even experienced social workers or PEs who are skilled and effective practitioners, and who are 'unconsciously competent', may, if they do not pay attention to their further learning needs, 'fall into poor habits' and thus become 'unconsciously incompetent'.

At the early stages of the placement, or at the 'unconscious incompetence' or 'conscious competence' stages, it may be helpful to consider the framework offered by Douglas (2008). He offers a framework that PEs can use to assess competence of the student before intervention and initial contact with service users. Although Douglas suggests using the framework to assess readiness for contact with service users, you may agree that it is also useful during the engagement stage and post-intervention with service users. The framework focuses the student's thinking and covers knowledge, skills and values and it can be used as a step-by-step approach or dipped into in a creative way. Douglas (2008) suggests that students consider the following seven areas.

1. *Legislation*

   What provides a mandate for intervention?

   What about statutory roles, responsibilities and requirements?

2. *Policy and procedures*

   What agency policies and procedures are relevant?

   How do they impact on, or direct this intervention?

3. *Theoretical considerations*

   Relating to this situation.

   Relating to method(s) of intervention.

4. *Previous knowledge*

   Held by agency/others.

   Student's experience of similar situations should be drawn on.

5. *Tuning in*

   To own feelings relating to this situation (self-awareness).

   To client's possible feelings concerning the agency, the student, the situation (preliminary empathy).

   To a strategy for intervention in the situation (purpose, beginning, contracting).

6. *Skills*

   What skills may be most relevant?

   Degrees of competence and confidence in using these?

7. *Values*

   What values and ethical issues are around in this situation?

   What are the implications for practice?

   Consider anti-oppressive practice issues.

Completing the exercise will provide the PE with an insight into the student's:

» competent use of English (this may appear basic, but this can highlight at an early stage if there are problematic issues);

» ability to locate and understand relevant legislation, policies and procedures;

» accuracy, breadth and depth of the knowledge base, and the capacity to make links between theory and practice;

» capacity to identify and draw on previous knowledge and experience, and the ability to transfer learning from other situations;

» ability to explore emotional and psychological aspects of people's experience, including their own;

» capacity to plan a contact with a service user which is purposive, sensitive and competent;

» understanding of social work values, the potential for oppression and constructive ways of dealing with issues;

» level of competence in core skills/attributes such as time management, information gathering, networking and perhaps even a capacity to take on board constructive criticism.

The Practice Curriculum

The PCF, as the professional framework, has a developmental focus and, at prequalifying level, recognises and expects that the student will develop their understanding and expertise in social work over the course of two placements. This will involve the PE in:

» structuring, planning and considering the learning opportunities across the placement and considering how they may be assessed;

» planning and considering each individual learning opportunity

Structuring and planning the learning opportunities across the placement involves considering what activities/opportunities are provided at what point in the placement; what is most relevant for the student and when; what has been negotiated/ agreed with the student at the Learning Agreement stage; and also considers the resources available within the agency. This is sometimes referred to as the Practice Curriculum and also includes the elements of pre-planning involved in the practice learning plan referred to in Chapter 3.

Shardlow and Doel (1996) consider ways in which learning can be structured through a Practice Curriculum on placement, in similar ways to the academic curriculum. They call for an explicit, written Practice Curriculum on placement which specifies clear aims and objectives for learning on placement; the detail of what the student will learn; the sequencing of the teaching/learning; the learning and teaching methods to be used; and how the learning/placement will be assessed. Many of these areas are incorporated in the initial Learning Agreements with students and have been referred to in Chapter 3. However, while most PEs will not have an explicit, written Practice

Curriculum, they should have a 'plan' in their heads; a *personal curriculum* (Shardlow and Doel, 1996, p. 96) for the placement which considers the learning opportunities across the placement and how these will be sequenced and structured, what should happen, when, and how. The PE can take the principles underlying Shardlow and Doel's (1996) 'explicit' Practice Curriculum on board by sharing and negotiating this with students as a way of both acknowledging the 'learning journey' of the student and the importance of student-centred learning. This will also assist PEs in meeting the PEPS (2013b) Domain B:4, B:6 and B:7.

Exercise: **the Practice Curriculum**

You can do this exercise on your own or with a student.

Consider some of the learning opportunities and areas of work that are available for the student within your setting. Then, map out how they link with the *required levels of the PCF* at either first or final level placement; finally, consider the particular complexity of each learning opportunity, what it involves, and thus at what point in the placement might each particular learning opportunity fit more suitably?

(This exercise will be also helpful in helping you prepare for the placement agreement meetings or mid-point reviews).

Area of work/learning opportunity	Links to which PCF domain?	At what point in the placement?

The PE's own development as an enabler

The PCF sets out that social workers have a professional responsibility to contribute to the development of the next generation of social workers, and undertaking the PE role is one way of doing this.

This book is aimed at PEs who are developing their learning in the role of PE and thus who are in the role as a 'teacher' and 'educator' at the same time as being a 'learner'. In order to undertake the role PEs need to be at least two years post qualified and considered to have expertise in their practice area. However, as Eraut (1994) notes, much of this knowledge and expertise will be *tacit knowledge* – professional knowledge and expertise that is largely inherent in the skills and attributes of the practitioner and informing their ways of working, but which is often invisible to them. One of the challenges for the PE then, in enabling the learning of a student, is to make their knowledge and understanding of the social work role *explicit*. This involves subjecting their knowledge to scrutiny and 'unpacking it', in order that they can then teach and facilitate the learning of another. For many PEs this is one of the chief reasons why they continue taking and supporting social work students – they recognise the value in both uncovering and 'unpacking' their understanding of the social work role and the skills and the knowledge embedded within it, as well as the opportunities that being a PE offers for reflection and further learning.

However, taking note of the key concepts underpinning learning outlined in this chapter, the PE needs support in their development as an enabler and some of the requirements regarding this will be discussed more fully in Chapter 9 on CPD. The Values for Practice Educators and supervisors, Value 7, and the PEPS (2013b) Domain D (for Stage 2 of the PEPS (2013b)) requires that PEs critically reflect on their professional development as a PE and part of this will be reflecting on the development of their skills in enabling. Some of the ways in which a PE can develop their enabling role is given below.

> » Seeking feedback from the student and/or university. All universities will have a quality assurance system that requires the student to give feedback on the placement and the PE. Further to this, the PE can ensure that seeking feedback from the student is an integral and ongoing element of the placement and part of the 'shared endeavour' of learning.

> » Seeking feedback, advice and guidance from a Stage 2 mentor or a colleague in workforce development or practice learning co-ordinator role. Feedback on your practice in supervision should be given as part of the direct observation of your practice required as part of the Stage 1 and Stage 2 requirements of the PEPS (2013b), but further help and guidance regarding facilitating student learning could be requested.

> » Co-delivery, or work with a more experienced PE or colleague, in relation to a particular teaching or facilitating strategy.

> » Seeking feedback and then self-evaluating by using the Professional Development prompt below.

> » Considering your further development needs and training or support that might be available. This may be in the form of university PE workshops or further training and opportunities negotiated by you as part of your CPD.

> ## Professional **development prompt: developing the PE as enabler**
>
> In light of some of the suggestions given in this chapter about how you might apply some enabling strategies/exercises with students, and taking into account your own learning style, consider the following.
>
> » How have I judged the success of my role as an enabler and facilitator of a student learner?
>
> » Which particular teaching/enabling strategies worked for me, and why?
>
> » What have been the highlights of the teaching /facilitating role for me?
>
> » What have I not felt so comfortable with?
>
> » Where can I go for further information, resources and training to help me with this aspect of my role?

Conclusion

This chapter has focused on the enabling and teaching elements of the PE role and what a PE can do to help facilitate student learning on placement. Key concepts under-pinning learning have been discussed, and exercises, teaching tools and strategies have been suggested which can help the PE in their enabling and teaching role. The importance of this role in meeting the requirements regarding the PEPS (2013b) and the PCF (2012) has been noted throughout this chapter. Further chapters – Chapter 5 on Supervision; Chapter 6 on Assessment and Chapter 8 on Reflective Practice pro-vide further information and guidance on the enabling elements of the PE role. Smith (2008) has noted that *learning is a process that is happening all the time; education involves intention and commitment*, and the aim of this chapter has been to encourage and facilitate the intention and commitment of those who are tasked with educating social work students on placement.

What does the research say?

Patricia Cartney's (2004) article in *Journal of Practice Teaching and Learning* 5(2), gives details of a small-scale study considering how PEs used an understanding of adult learning theory and Honey and Mumford's (1992) 'Learning Styles Questionnaire' (LSQ) in teaching and working with their social work students on placement.

The sample included eight PEs and their respective students. At the beginning of placement, each PE completed the LSQ to ascertain their learning style. They then worked in a group with others of a similar learning style (Activists; Pragmatists; Reflectors or Theorists) to consider how they learned best and what teaching methods they preferred. From this group exercise they devised a Learning Code for each type of student learner, suggesting teaching and learning activities the PE could provide to help particular learners most fully utilise the learning opportunities on placement. The Learning Code for each type of learner is detailed below.

Each of the respective students was asked to complete the LSQ at beginning of placement.

At the end of placement, PEs and students were interviewed to see how PEs' knowledge and understanding of adult learning styles and the Learning Code they had devised had influenced the placement.

Key messages highlighted in the research

» PEs and students found the knowledge around their LSQ useful.

» PEs used and incorporated their understanding and use of LSQ in the placement in 3 different ways.

1. *Developmentally* – information gained from student and PE completion of LSQ was integrated into the placement learning throughout and learning opportunities were influenced and informed as a result of this.

2. *Diagnostically* – where problems in learning had been identified, LSQs was used as part of action planning and resolution.

3. *Dilatory* – information about learning styles had been sought but as an end in itself and not acted upon or been incorporated into teaching during the placement.

» Usefulness of undertaking the LSQ is more determined by how the information is used to inform learning on placement; it is most helpful if used *developmentally* to provide a framework for teaching and learning on placement.

Learning Code suggested for each type of learner

Reflector

» Stressed need for time and space.

» Need to provide opportunities for observing others before undertaking tasks alone.

» Provide reflective supervision with time to discuss process/outcomes/ potential outcomes and actions.

» Suggest reading material to be discussed at next supervision to allow thinking time prior to discussion.

» Provide encouragement to move to action as the end product of reflection – ie action plans; timescales on supervision notes.

Pragmatist

» The importance of problem solving and utilising 'what works'.

» Provide opportunities for problem solving and planning – could be in relation to casework, projects, specific issues, etc.

» Provide opportunities to see different ways of working – eg, co-working with colleagues with varied work styles, specialisms, etc.

» Provide opportunities for the student to 'see the wood for the trees'; use supervision to help the student reflect on how their work fitted with wider issues (societal, structural) and make connections between their discrete tasks and the wider picture.

» In supervision, provide opportunities for the student to put theoretical ideas into practice – eg, one particular piece of work could be looked at from a variety of different perspectives and the pros and cons of each explored.

Theorist

» Need for a clear, organised teaching framework stressed.

» Provide a structured and organised plan for both induction and placement process showing how the visits/work undertaken links to the student's identified learning needs.

» Provide opportunities to link theories to practice in supervision, in relation to different cases, etc.; how the parts link with the whole.

» Provide encouragement that it is okay not to know all the answers – discussions on the possibility of 'safe uncertainty'.

Activist

» Need for learning through 'hands on' experience.

» Provide accelerated induction packages with quick movement to performing tasks rather than observing, etc.

» Provide varied learning experiences which are outlined at the contract stage.

» Provide opportunities to initiate and become involved in new projects and pieces of work.

» Provide opportunities to slow down and reflect – may be needed but will not be initiated by the student – eg, by asking them in supervision to consider the pros and cons of a range of differing alternative courses before moving to an action plan.

(Cartney, P. (2004), pp. 51–72)

Taking it further

Shardlow, S. and Doel, M. (1996) *Practice Learning and Teaching*, Hampshire: Macmillan Press. This is a classic text, and Chapter 4 on 'Understanding Learning' and Chapter 5 on 'Using a curriculum for Practice Learning' are particularly helpful.

Beverley, A. and Worsley, A. (2007) *Learning and Teaching in Social Work Practice*, Hampshire: Palgrave. A really helpful, easy-to-read and understand introduction to many of the themes and concepts regarding learning and teaching in this chapter; particularly Chapter 3 on 'Adult Learning' and Chapter 4 on 'Creating and Using Learning Opportunities'.

Cree, V. (2005) Students learning to learn, in Burgess, H. and Taylor, I. (eds) (2005) *Effective Learning and Teaching in Social Policy and Social Work*, London: Routledge Palmer. More detailed explanation of the concept of 'learning to learn'.

Thompson, N. (2006) *Promoting Workplace Learning*, Bristol: Policy Press. A practical text, offering guidance and strategies for practice learning and also wider aspects of coaching and mentoring. Chapter 1 on 'Understanding Learning' and Chapter 2 on 'Teaching and Assessing Values' are particularly helpful.

Cartney, P. (2000) 'Adult Learning Styles: Implications for practice teaching in social work' in *Social Work Education*, 19(6): 609–26 – small-scale study of adult learning styles and the implications for work with students.

Bartoli, A. *et al.* (2013) *Anti-racism in Social Work Practice*, Northwich: Critical Publishing. Includes Prospera Tedam's MANDELA model.

Chapter 5 | Supervision

The material in this chapter links to the following PE Professional Standards and values statements for PEs and supervisors:

Learning outcome domains required for Stage 1 and Stage 2 PEs

A:1; A:4; A:7; A:8; B:1; B:2; B:3; B:5; B:6; B:7; B:8; B:9; C:1; C:9

Additional learning outcome domains required for Stage 2 PEs

B:10; D:1; D:6

Values for PEs and supervisors: 1, 3 and 7

Chapter aims

» To consider the role of supervision in the development of professional practice – for the student and for the PE.

» To consider the main functions of student supervision and how they link to facilitating student reflection and learning.

» To consider different models of supervision and how they may be applied in supervision with a student.

» To examine how supervision should be structured and what skills, techniques and approaches are helpful for PEs to use during supervision.

» To consider issues of power differentials within supervision.

Critical **questions**

» How will I maintain the balance between the differing functions of supervision – to ensure that the needs of the service user and the learning and developmental needs of the student are both met?

» How do I ensure that I use the power and authority in my role of supervisor in a professional manner and demonstrate anti-oppressive values?

» How can my own professional supervision be extended to incorporate and support my role as a supervisor and PE of social work students?

Introduction: the role of reflective supervision

Supervision plays an essential role within the placement – it is a key site of learning for the student and where their professional identity as a social worker matures; it is where the relationship between the student and the PE is embedded; and it is the arena where the many and varied roles of a PE – the support, education and management functions of the placement – converge. As Lord Laming (2003) notes: *Effective supervision is the cornerstone of safe social work practice. There is no substitute for it* (p. 211). Those who write about supervision and authors of recent reports about social work (Laming, 2003; Laming, 2009; CWDC, 2009; Munro, 2011; Wonnacott, 2012) are clear about its essential role in providing a space for direction, support, reflection and guidance for the worker and thus its contribution to effective practice and better outcomes for service users. However, despite its long tradition and essential role in social work, successive reports (Laming, 2003; Laming, 2009; Munro, 2011; DfE, 2009) have highlighted that many social workers and student social workers have received inadequate, poor quality supervision and that supervision has often been dominated by 'managerial' demands. In particular, the recent *Social Work Taskforce Final report* (DfE, 2009) brought the issue of effective supervision to the fore, noting that supervision for both social workers and students needs to be *high quality, reflective supervision* (p. 31) and one of the 15 recommendations of the SWTF has resulted in national standards for supervision and the Standards for Employers of Social Workers in England and Supervision Framework. (See SWRB/LGA, undated).

Thus supervision has an enhanced role and mandate within current social work, and it is within this context that the pivotal role of the PE within student supervision will be discussed in this chapter. However, while the emphasis will be on how the PE can provide effective supervision for a social work student, it should not be forgotten that supervision will also be the location where many PEs will be observed in their practice as part of the requirements for meeting the PEPS Stage 1 or Stage 2. Further consideration will be given to this in Chapter 9.

A note on the definition of 'supervision'

For our purposes in this chapter, when we refer to 'supervision' we are referring to formal, planned supervision sessions taking place on a one-to-one basis between the PE and the student. A useful definition is provided by Ford and Jones (1987, p.63): *By supervision, we mean planned, regular periods of time that a student and supervisor spend together discussing the student's work in the placement and reviewing the learning progress*. Ford and Jones (1987) differentiate this formal supervision from 'consultation' – which the student may seek on an ad hoc basis from the PE or other members of the team. This 'consultation' usually has a problem-solving focus and is also sometimes referred to as 'informal supervision'. Such 'informal supervision' will necessarily take place during the placement, but it is important that it does not become the dominant form of PE and student interaction; also it is essential that any decisions taken or advice given 'informally' are then referred to and recorded during the next supervision.

There are other forms of supervision, such as group supervision and peer supervision, but these are not the focus of this chapter. References and further reading in relation to these forms of supervision will be given at the end of this chapter.

'Getting it right': first steps

Although all PEs will have experienced supervision in the role of supervisee, for many PEs supervising a social work student is their first experience of supervision *in the role of supervisor*. This can be both an exciting prospect – in the experience of the authors many of the PEs we have trained comment positively on the training day within the course that looks at the functions of supervision, and enjoy the 'uncovering' of knowledge and ideas for structuring supervision, and the skills used in supervision – but also a challenging one. As a PE you will want to 'get it right' – you will be keen to ensure that your student is accountable and carrying out your agency functions properly so that the benefit, well-being and safety of service users is ensured, but you will also be aware that student supervision should be a place for reflection and development and that providing a forum for this is also an important part of your role. It was noted in Chapter 3 that the supervisory relationship is a key sphere of influence for the PE and one that helps establish a positive learning environment for the student. Effective planning and preparation for the supervisory element of your role is crucial; for example, prior to the student's arrival you will need to consider how you will manage your time and how you will diarise supervision – where and when it will take place; what supervision recording pro-formas you might use; and how your student's direct work with service users/casework will be recorded on any systems within your agency. Your preparation should also include some time spent considering how the supervisory relationship will be influenced by your own experiences of supervision as a supervisee. By giving thought to this, and acknowledging these influences, you will be demonstrating the importance of the Values for PEs and supervisors, in particular the origin and impact of your values and assumptions and your views on the use of authority within the role.

The Supervision Agreement

The supervisory relationship will also be influenced by the previous experiences of the student, either from their prior working life or their first placement. Thus, a shared understanding of the purpose of supervision by both parties is key. As was discussed in Chapter 3, the concept of supervision should be introduced at the very beginning of the placement (during induction) and a useful starting point could be to discuss similar areas as those within the professional development prompt above with the student and explore previous experiences with them and their thoughts on the role and purpose of supervision. Beyond their previous experiences, good quality supervision also needs to take into account the student's existing skills and strengths; their learning needs and areas for development; and their learning style. The completion of a Supervision Agreement at the first supervision session can be used to facilitate a discussion of these issues, to highlight the centrality of supervision and to underline a shared understanding of the purpose of supervision. It can also set the tone for the supervisory relationship – which is a partnership where collaborative working is central and the student is expected to be an active participant. A Supervision Agreement usually involves the following:

» timing, regularity and location of supervision;

» recording of supervision notes;

» how interruptions/cancellations/rearrangements will be dealt with;

» expectations and professional responsibilities on both sides regarding the role of supervision; content of the sessions and preparation and planning involved;

» confidentiality and its limits;

» power and authority issues and further recourse/sources of support available to the student.

A sample Supervision Agreement is provided in Appendix 1.

Functions of supervision

Doel (2010) suggests that there are four related but separate elements to social work student supervision, which he refers to as ESMA.

1. Education function
2. Support function
3. Management function
4. Assessment function

This view of student supervision extends the classic view of the three functions of social work supervision offered by Kadushin (1976) – the administrative/managerial; educative and supportive functions. These functions are often expressed as the corners of an equilateral triangle, each of the component parts having equal 'weight' and importance. It is clear how each of these three functions relate to the main areas of the PE role as outlined in Chapter 3 – support, management of the placement and the education and teaching element of the PE role, but it is also important to remember how supervision contributes to the assessment of the student – which will be discussed in greater detail in Chapter 6.

Professional **development prompt**

» Consider three of the functions of supervision – the education, management and support functions. What 'weight' should be given to each?

» How will you ensure that the 'managerial' considerations do not dominate?

Management function

This function of supervision is concerned with the 'quality assurance' aspect of a placement and ensuring that the student is working in accordance with national standards and legislation and any agency policy and procedures. The key aim of this function is to safeguard the protection and safety of service users and carers. This will involve ensuring the student's accountability for their work on placement and their understanding and adherence to agency requirements – for example, in relation to key processes; case recording requirements; safeguarding; and health and safety. The 'managerial' aspect in relation to supervision of a student also relates to the management of the placement itself and managing the demands of both the professional framework that the student is working within and the educational institution – for example, working with the student to help them understand their assessment and placement portfolio requirements; and agreeing with the student key objectives to be met by certain points in the placement. In doing the latter you will be meeting many of the requirements of Domain B of the PEPS (2013b) – for example, B:2, B:3 and B:4.

Support function

Supervision should be a source of support for students, as an arena for managing the emotional impact of working with vulnerable people and also where the student can receive support in managing the demands of their professional training and the university/placement/assessment portfolio/life balance. Supervision should be a place where students can be helped to recognise and acknowledge the emotional stresses of working with vulnerable or challenging service users. However, the supportive function of supervision extends beyond the attention given to the well-being of the worker/student, and as O'Sullivan (2010) reminds us, supervision also plays a role in promoting positive outcomes for service users as supportive supervision *should include helping the worker develop his or her thinking about the case* (p. 162). In relation to student supervision there are some further issues that PEs need to be aware of – professional and supervisory boundaries, and 'fears' and barriers to effective support.

Professional and supervisory boundaries

Doel (2009) refers to the support element of supervision as the *grey area* which is *frequently spoken of in general, vague terms* (p. 110) and that PEs have to be mindful of professional and supervisory boundaries. He reminds PEs that supervision is *not therapy*. If the emotional impact of the work with service users is experienced as overwhelming, or if the student has personal issues that are impacting on the placement, they can be acknowledged and discussed to a degree during supervision; but any further help, support or counselling required has to be accessed outside the placement. The student and the PE must also be mindful of the requirements of both the HCPC *Guidance on Conduct and Ethics for Students* (2012d), which require the student to acknowledge and limit or stop their studies if their performance or judgement is affected by their health. Any situation such as this will need to be managed sensitively by the PE and the student's tutor/the university involved. Similarly, if the student is struggling with the demands of their academic work – either that which is expected within the placement portfolio or academic assignments outside the portfolio – and balancing this with the demands of the placement, this can be acknowledged within supervision. While the PE can be supportive and often give some help and advice regarding issues such as time management or the theoretical underpinnings and knowledge required to help with academic assignments, care must be taken that supervision is not dominated by these issues. The student should be encouraged to seek further support from their tutor or specific support services offered within the university.

'Fears' and barriers to effective support

Davys and Beddoe (2010) note that there can be barriers to the exploration of feelings within supervision that can stem from three fears, which they characterise as fear of being overwhelmed by feelings; fear of the judgement of others; and fear of distortion within the professional encounter. It is worthwhile considering how these fears may be manifested in the placement setting – for both students and PEs – and how they might be managed. For the student, emotional feelings may be perceived as adding to anxiety or pressure already associated with the placement, and they may be suppressed in favour of a desire to simply 'get on with the placement and pass'; feelings may be perceived by students as a sign of weakness or evidence of 'over involvement' or, being conscious of the value base of social work, they may feel uncomfortable about sharing strong negative feelings about service users or their lifestyles believing that they or their practice will be judged adversely. Students are also acutely aware that they are being assessed on their placement and can avoid mentioning anything that would suggest they may be struggling with any aspect of practice or professional development. It may also be that students do not feel safe in the supervision relationship or feel that the supervisor will not respond appropriately if discussions of the emotional impact of the work have not been encouraged or modelled by the PE. For the PE, a reluctance to address feelings within supervision can stem from feeling overwhelmed by the demands of the role, coupled as it often is with a busy caseload, or the PE may feel inadequately supported in the role within their own supervision and agency. In such a situation, a 'caseload management' approach that purely concentrates on the 'work to be done' can seem achievable. The PE may also fear exposing inadequacies as a PE – for many PEs, supervision of a student is their first experience in the role of supervisor and this in itself can cause anxiety as they are in a role of authority and can feel that they need to 'know all the answers'. Even where PEs have had previous students, each student will present different needs and styles and some may have particular learning needs or difficulties which need to be managed, which may be new for the PE.

Supervision should be a source of support for students with the chief aim of guiding their professional development while ensuring effective and safe work with service users. Wonnacott (2012) puts this simply – *supervision needs to provide a forum for consideration of feelings, thoughts and actions* (p. 36). For student supervision we would also add that this has to take place within a boundaried supervisory relationship where the needs of the service user remain paramount.

Education function

This is the function of supervision that is concerned with learning and the development of professional competence and which, particularly for student supervision, should have enhanced emphasis. McKitterick (2012, p. 21) suggests that supervision is a key place for learning and there are four elements of learning required within the supervision process.

1. Reflection and thoughtful, shared, critical analysis of available information, the review of intuitive judgements and of relevant research evidence.

2. Gaining knowledge, including the ability to evaluate research on what works, and reviewing formal training received.

3. Development of practice skills to intervene as a social worker to achieve change.

4. Development of the ability to process complex information and knowledge, to cogently analyse and to express in written and verbal communication.

McKitterick (2012) here is referring to the supervision of social workers but each of these four elements can be extended and 'reworked' to have particular relevance to the learning required by students to meet with the relevant student levels of the PCF domains and which need to be facilitated within supervision. These are given below.

1. *Reflection and critical analysis of practice* – reflection is the subject of Chapter 8 and the role of supervision in facilitating thoughtful and critical reflection on practice is also the focus of one of the models of supervision referred to later in this chapter (see Davys and Beddoe, 2010). Supervision is the key location for consideration of PCF Domain 6 – *critical reflection*

and analysis – apply critical reflection and analysis to inform and provide a rationale for professional decision making ... apply imagination, creativity and curiosity to practice. Supervision should also be a place where students are encouraged to examine their values (within a safe and supportive environment) and above all, where self-awareness is encouraged, thus considering the implications of PCF Domain 2 – *Values and Ethics: apply social work ethical principles and values to guide professional practice ... recognise and, with support, manage the impact of own values on professional practice.* As the PE you can support the student in this through feedback – good practice guidance on this is in Chapter 4 on 'Enabling learning'.

2. *Gaining, using knowledge and evaluating research and formal training received* – supervision is clearly a forum where the PE will be involved in 'teaching' and providing knowledge and information. This may be explaining and demonstrating a particular method of working pertinent to the agency or providing information and explaining a new policy or procedure. As the PE, part of your role here is also to facilitate the student's understanding of how theoretical knowledge (the theories and methods; the wider underpinning knowledge and socio-economic context of practice) taught in the academic setting apply to practice and direct work with service users. Students should be encouraged to name, apply and critique the underpinning knowledge they have gained from their academic studies. Supervision thus plays an essential part in consideration of PCF Domain 5 – *Knowledge: Apply knowledge of social sciences, law and social work practice theory.* Within the PE role, the 'didactic' (teaching) element is intertwined with the 'facilitative' element and as a PE you will need to manage the tension between these two elements.

3. *Development of practice skills* – the placement is a key arena for the development of practice skills as it offers the unique opportunity to work with service users, one-to-one, or in group settings, and to apply and hone communication and direct work skills. Within the PCF emphasis is given to the development of skills and 'applied frameworks' of practice – PCF Domain 7 – *Intervention and skills: use judgement and authority to intervene with individuals, families and communities ... select and use appropriate frameworks to assess, plan, implement and review effective outcomes.* Current requirements for social work training also feature a '30 days skills development' component, delivered within the university but with an expected input from practitioners and agency partners, some days of which will be delivered before the student begins placement and further days which will be delivered throughout the degree course. The placement

will give the student the chance to apply and develop skills taught within these '30 days'. Supervision can be used to help students in this task – for example, in simulation of activities; rehearsal of interventions; discussion and planning of appropriate methods.

4. *Processing complex information and knowledge, analysing and developing written and verbal communication abilities* – the processing and analysis of complex information – 'being able to see the wood for the trees' – is an important developmental task for a social work student. The expectation that a social work student should be able to manage complexity, prioritise appropriately and work more autonomously is embedded within the PCF requirements for the final placement. Similarly, with regard to the student's developing verbal and written communication abilities, as the PE you should have an oversight of the student's case recording or other written records, as this is an essential part of the 'administrative/managerial' aspect of your role. You can use supervision to study – with the student – elements of the student's recordings (perhaps alongside your own) and consider strengths and/or identify areas for improvement and how they might be achieved.

Later in this chapter we will look at skills, techniques and questioning prompts that can be used by the PE during supervision to assist in these learning and facilitative tasks.

Many recent reports – Laming, 2009; Munro, 2011 and the *SWTF Final report* (DfE, 2009) – have noted that much of professional social work supervision has been dominated by a 'managerial' focus entailing meeting targets and performance criteria. Morrison and Wonnacott (2010) name this supervision as *compliance checking rather than exploration of practice* that has been *to the detriment of reflection, critical analysis and emotional support for the worker.* However, just as they feel that the current social work reform agenda presents a unique opportunity to *reclaim reflective supervision* for all social workers, so PEs must also ensure that the balance is maintained between the managerial/administrative demands of the placement and the opportunities that supervision provides for enabling, teaching and learning and a 'reflective space' for the student. The provision of 'reflective supervision' and the emphasis on the student developing an overall understanding of their role and interventions via critical analysis and the application of knowledge and thinking to their practice, also supports holistic assessment and will provide important foundations for the PE's professional judgement and final assessment of the student. This will be considered in further detail in Chapter 6 on 'Assessment'.

Models of supervision – newer developments

The 'traditional' model of supervision as offered by Kadushin (1976), that outlines the three main functions of supervision, has been criticised by Morrison and Wonnacott (2010) for viewing the functions as separate rather than interactive and for not identifying the role of the supervisor in facilitating critical analysis of practice. Further, there are important features of supervision that are essential for PEs to be aware of and which will inform their work with social work students.

» *The context of supervision* – both Morrison (2001) and Tsui (2005) remind us that supervision takes place within a *particular context* and that it is not simply a relationship between two people but is a *multifaceted relationship* (Tsui, 2005, p. 41) that involves the supervisor, the supervisee, the service user, the agency and the wider cultural context. For PEs the *context* also involves the team, the university and the wider requirements of the PCF as the occupational framework within which both student and PE are operating. The additional 'person in the room' for the PE is also the PEPS (2013b) and the requirements of assessment that it imposes on PEs.

» *Supervision is part of the intervention with service users* (Morrison and Wonnacott, 2010, p. 5) – this is a powerful and important message and should underlie all the work of supervision and highlights not only the centrality of the service user within supervision but the necessity of supervision. For both students and PEs then, supervision is not an 'optional extra' – it is part of the work students undertake with service users and the outcomes for service users will be detrimentally affected if effective, regular and thoughtful supervision does not take place.

Here we will turn to a consideration of two more recent models of supervision that may be helpful for PEs in their work with students on placement. Domain B:10 of the PEPS (2013b) requires that to achieve Stage 2 PEs can apply a range of supervisory models and skills.

The Reflective Learning Model

(Davys and Beddoe, 2010; Davys and Beddoe, 2009)

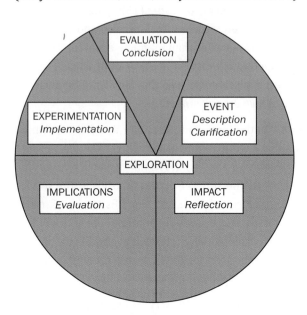

© Davys, A and Beddoe, L (2009) The Reflective Learning Model: Supervision of Social Work Students. *Social Work Education: The International Journal*, 28(8): 919–33

This model focuses on the *process* of supervision and describes a four stage cycle of supervision that closely follows Kolb's (1984) cycle of experiential learning (referred to in Chapter 4 Enabling Learning) with specific tasks at each stage for supervisor and supervisee. The authors feel that this model will help promote reflection (the '*exploration*') but also, in moving to the 'experimentation' stage ('*will this work?*') and the 'evaluation' stage ('*what are we agreeing needs to be done to make this work?*') conclusions are reached and further action is highlighted. The stages comprise the following.

» *The Event* – where the student is encouraged to explain the 'event' or interaction with the service user in order that both the supervisor and supervisee gain a clear understanding of the issue

» *The Exploration* – this is the stage where the authors believe that the 'work' of supervision takes place and is divided into 2 phases – discussing the impact of the event on the student and exploring the students own role in it before moving onto the second phase of exploration, the implications. This involves the student and PE together considering the 'case' more broadly and the legislation, policies and theories that can inform and guide future action; the aim here is increased understanding, insight and knowledge.

Davys and Beddoe (2009) suggest that this phase enables the PE to gauge the level of the student's knowledge and understanding and is the phase *where the supervisor is most active and where he or she has the opportunity to teach, inform and prescribe* (p. 927).

» *Experimentation* – this is the implementation stage where the plan or strategy is tested – will it work? What resources does the student need in order to implement this plan?

» *The Evaluation* – this is the stage where the PE checks out with the student that they have understood what has been agreed; that they have enough resources and confidence to put the plan into action and time frames are agreed. When this stage has been completed, the student and PE will focus on the next agenda item and begin the cycle once more.

Beyond its use as a model of supervision, this model may also help students in preparing any written critically reflective analyses of their practice within their placement portfolios.

The 4x4x4 Integrated Model of Supervision

(Morrison and Wonnacott, 2010; CWDC, 2009)

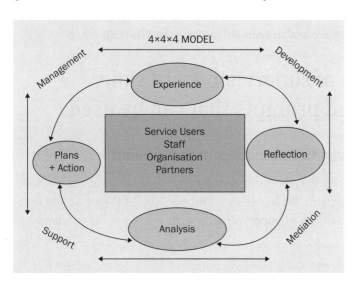

Morrison and Wonnacott (2010) suggest that this model of supervision recognises the complexity of supervision and takes into account the range of tasks, stakeholders and functions that are interconnected within supervision. It places supervision in its wider context and also has a focus on the process of supervision itself. The model has been developed for (qualified) social workers and is explained below and adapted to address a student placement.

> » *The four stakeholders in supervision – the middle circle.* The four stakeholders are at the centre of supervision and their needs and priorities are always kept in mind. They include the service user, staff (the supervisee/supervisor or student and PE), the agency/organisation, and other external agencies or partners in the process (these will be other agencies but for student supervision will also include the university and the professional requirements of the PCF and the HCPC).

> » *The four elements of the supervisory cycle – the 'second' circle.* Again, and similarly to Davys and Beddoe (2009; 2010) above, this element of the 4x4x4 model focuses on the *process* of supervision itself and closely follows Kolb's (1984) of experiential learning. This is called the 'reflective supervision cycle' and it is described as *the glue that holds the model together* (Wonnacott, 2012, p. 54). Within supervision, the student should be encouraged to 'tell the story'; to reflect; to analyse and understand; and to identify further goals and plans.

> » *The four functions of supervision* – These are some of the familiar functions previously discussed; named as management, development (education), support and mediation. The mediation function is noted as engaging the individual with the wider agency.

Further details of this model can also be found in Wonnacott (2012).

The structure of supervision and skills, techniques and prompts that can be used

Structure of supervision throughout the placement

Similarly to the way in which the placement is structured, supervision also has a structure throughout the placement. Walker *et al.* (2008, pp. 108–111) give a good overview of this and their structure of supervision through the life of the placement is adapted here.

Beginning

The necessity for effective planning and preparation for your role as supervisor and the need to agree a Supervision Contract has been referred to earlier in this chapter. Part of your planning and preparation will involve:

» Considering the work that can be allocated to the student. This involves thinking through what activities or opportunities for learning can be provided and at what point in the placement; what is most relevant for the student and when; and what are the relevant PCF student level descriptors for this placement. Much of this will have been addressed at the Learning Agreement meeting.

» Planning for the supervision sessions. This involves considering where supervision will take place (a room or setting is preferable where you can have supervision undisturbed); the process and timing of supervision; how you will make time for it in your diary; and how each supervision session will be structured. You also have to spend some time thinking about how you hope to establish a supportive, working relationship – this means modelling reflective and anti-oppressive practice yourself, being familiar with the university requirements and the student's own learning styles and needs.

Middle

This is what Walker *et al.* (2008) call the *core phase* and is where the *working alliance* (p. 110) with the student should be established. The student should be working with a number of service users, building on knowledge and developing key skills appropriate to their level of training and the student level requirements of the PCF. Feedback from the PE and dialogue between student and PE should have been a regular feature of supervision and, if there are any issues regarding the student's performance or development, these should be raised with the student. The middle of the placement is also the phase where there is a formal 'mid-point' review of the student's progress and where decisions are made regarding further learning opportunities available and required before the end of the placement. Planning for 'endings' – for the student and for the student's work with service users – also begins during the 'middle' phase.

End

This involves considering ending the work the student has carried out with service users and within the agency, and entails ensuring that all relevant paperwork, case recordings or 'handovers' are completed. This is an important focus, but care must be taken to ensure that this is not rushed or that it dominates the process of 'endings' for the student and PE. The emotional response to the ending of the placement must also be considered. As PEs, the authors are familiar with a whole range of emotions felt by PEs and students alike (often all at the same time) – relief; sadness; happiness at a job well done; frustration at not being able to 'see things through'; anticipation of 'what next?' or thoughts of 'have I done enough?' If a placement has not run smoothly or if the outcome has not been successful, particular feelings of disappointment, anger, frustration or doubt might be present. It is essential not only to review the work completed with a student during the placement but also for the student and PE to consider the student's 'next stage' in their journey, which may be the next and final placement or the stage of qualification. The PE can ask the student to consider their progress by answering the following questions – *where was I at the beginning?*; *where am I now and what have I learnt?*; *what are my future learning needs and objectives?*. This encourages student self-assessment and in so doing, enhances the contribution to their development and assessment and maximises the sharing of power within the assessment process (see Chapter 6 on 'Assessment'). Acknowledgement and thanks for the student's work within the team is also an important part of endings and is often marked by a card, or a team outing, or other such 'ending ritual'.

Professional **development prompt**

The importance of 'endings' also applies to the PE. Towards the end of the placement it is useful for the PE to consider their own development and ask themselves the same questions as those posed above for the student:

» Where was I at the beginning of the student's placement?

» Where am I now and what have I learnt?

» What are my future learning needs and objectives?

Self-evaluation is sound practice for all PEs but for those PEs undertaking Stage 2 of the PEPS, it is a requirement of Domain D (TCSW, 2013b, p. 10) that PEs *critically reflect and evaluate their own professional development and apply learning to subsequent practice education experience using a range of methods.*

Skills, techniques and prompts used in supervision

As a PE you will be using an array of skills, interventions, questioning techniques and prompts with students during supervision. Many of these skills and techniques of intervention are those which you will be using in your work as a social worker with service users, but an awareness of them in relation to your role in assisting a student's development is also required and can help fulfil the requirements of Stage 2, Domain B:10 of the PEPS.

Given the range of tasks involved in the PE role, it is clear that PEs need a combination of skills and that particularly within supervision PEs need to use skills of engagement, challenge, support and clarification, as the following diagram illustrates.

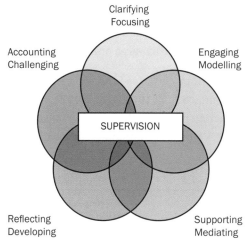

(Model taken from CWDC 2009, p. 47)

Heron (1975, as outlined in Hawkins and Shohet, 2006, p. 135) divided interventions in any facilitating or enabling process into six categories of intervention, which he felt were *authoritative* or *facilitative*.

Authoritative	Prescriptive	Give advice, be directive – eg, you will need to write a referral to ...; you will need to write a report on that ...
	Informative	Be didactic, instruct, inform – eg, you will find a similar report in X file ...; this is how our recording system works ...
	Confrontative	Be challenging; give direct feedback – eg, I notice when you talk about X you seem angry/you smile ... This should be constructive challenge, to help the student consider behaviour or attitudes of which they might be unaware.
Facilitative	Cathartic	What is it you really want to say? eg, help the student to express thoughts or emotions.
	Catalytic	Be reflective, encourage self-directed problem solving – eg, can you say some more about that? How can you do that?
	Supportive	Be affirming and acknowledge the student's competences, qualities and achievements; offer praise.

As a PE it is always helpful to begin a supervision session with a *How are you?*, and, after a brief discussion arising from this, ask *What would you like on the agenda?*. The rest of the session will usually involve a mixture of 'authoritative' and 'facilitative' interventions on the part of the PE, and the balance between them can be dependent on the particular stage of the placement or the learning needs of the student – for example, interventions may be more 'authoritative', directive or informative during the early stages of the placement or when allocating a particular area or piece of work.

Closely related to the four stages of the supervisory cycle (see the 4x4x4 Model of Supervision as outlined by Morrison and Wonnacott, 2010; CWDC, 2009) and the stages of experience, reflection, analysis and action planning, these authors also offer some helpful questions to guide the supervisor/PE in using the supervision cycle with students to discuss work with service users.

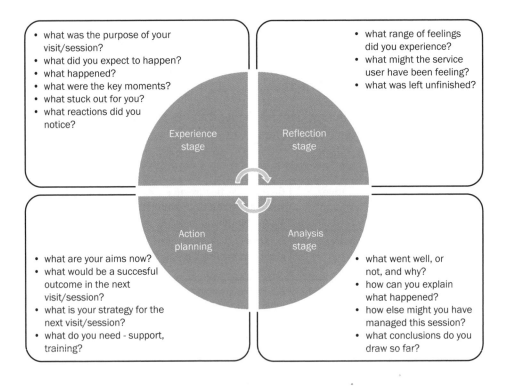

A fuller list of questions around the supervisory cycle is available in CWDC (2009) *NQSW: guide for supervisors: newly qualified social worker pilot programme 2009–2010*, Appendix 3.

Exercise

You are in a supervision session with Debra, a student who is mid-way through her final 100-day placement in a Local Authority children and families team. She has been to visit the Greene family following an incident where their 14-year-old daughter Susan recently left the family home after an argument and is now staying with a friend, refusing to return. Debra visited Susan in school and Susan had told her that there had been a family argument about her being rude and staying out late, and she had walked out in response. She had stayed two nights at a friend's house and was refusing to return home, although not giving many reasons other than saying her parents were always shouting at her and that she had had enough. Debra has just been to visit Susan's parents, Mr and Mrs Greene. In response to your inquiry about how the visit went, Debra replies as below.

Task

Read her response and consider what questions you could ask Debra to take her round the 'supervisory cycle' and to find out more about her reflections, to prompt her thinking and her next steps. Use some of the reflective questions and prompts suggested in the previous model.

Debra's response

The visit was just awful! Mr and Mrs Greene were there and also Mr Greene's mother – Susan's gran, Mrs Brown, although she doesn't live with them – but she did most of the talking. I was trying to ask Mr and Mrs Greene what the argument with Susan had been about as I hadn't got much detail from Susan, just that she was adamant she wasn't going to return home. The grandmother, Mrs Brown, started shouting that Susan was no good, ungrateful and cheeky and that her son had a weak heart and health problems and he wasn't even Susan's real dad anyway. Mrs Brown said she was there when Susan had started the argument with her dad and that she had told Susan 'I don't know why you're shouting at him, he's not your real dad anyway, go and argue with him if you can find him'. I asked if Susan had known this before and Mrs Greene said no, they had never told Susan as Mr Greene had brought her up since she was a baby. Mrs Brown started really shouting then, saying it was about time she knew anyway, that she was sick of the way her son was treated by Susan, and then Mrs Greene started crying, saying 'you always bring this up ... I've never been good enough for you'. Mr Greene then stood up and said he had had enough of all the problems this was causing and he left the room. Mrs Greene was really crying by this point and said to me: 'Now can you see all the problems I've got? I'm depressed enough as it is without all this ... '

I was just sitting in the middle of it all. There didn't seem to be anything I could say or do that wouldn't make the situation worse.

Mrs Brown then stormed out saying that I was just wasting time and that Susan should stay where she was; that she'd been spoilt rotten by Mrs Greene and that she was not her son's problem anymore. I stayed for a bit longer until Mrs Greene had calmed down. It seems as though she does want Susan to return but not yet; she wanted 'things to calm down at home first' and said she didn't know how to handle things with Susan now she knew about her dad ... I just feel I didn't get very far ... I feel awful about it, it was just a mess!

It is important to remember that supervision should be a *dialogue* and that these questions and prompts can be used as tools to *encourage student engagement* in the supervision session and not as either an 'inquisition' or a 'question/answer session'. If you feel supervision is turning into the latter, either with you continually posing 'questions' and the student giving limited 'answers', or, if the student asks a lot of 'questions' and expects you to have all the 'answers' and be entirely directive throughout each session, then you need to acknowledge, discuss and address this with the student. You can refer back to the Supervision Agreement with the student and reiterate the expectations regarding collaborative working and the student's contribution to supervision. You can also remind the student of relevant professional requirements – the HCPC *Guidance on conduct and ethics for students*, Standard 6 (HCPC, 2012d) specifically requires that the student takes responsibility for their own learning; similarly, the requirements of the PCF places a responsibility on the student to understand, apply and achieve the domain levels.

Power and authority in supervision

Wonnacott (2012; 2013) uses the term *authoritative supervision* as the ideal style of the effective supervisor; an 'authoritative supervisor' being clear about expectations and practice standards but also able to work effectively with relationships and provide the type of safe and enabling environment that we have been referring to in this chapter. Further, any discussion of the PE role is incomplete without a consideration of the power and authority within the PE role.

Brown and Bourne (1996) suggest that the supervisory relationship is influenced by two types of power – formal and informal power. Within the student/PE relationship, the PE has formal power and authority embedded in the role – they are the ultimate assessor of the student and it is their holistic assessment of the student, based on their professional judgement, which will determine if the student passes or fails the placement. Informal power is that which derives from the PE's personal attributes and their professional knowledge and skills and status as a qualified social worker. Brown and Bourne (1996) also remind us that the informal power of both supervisor and supervisee derives from *the structurally determined identities and roles based on key characteristics like race, gender, class, age, sexual orientation and (dis)ability* (p. 39) Such structural determinants of informal power – and the hidden assumptions or unspoken manifestations that can apply as a result of them – can exert a powerful influence on the placement and the supervision process, and the PE (and student) need to think about and recognise where they may be apparent. Akhtar (2013) notes the influence that factors such as *being 'other'* or *being the 'same'* (p. 137) can have on supervision – that is, being 'other' can lead to differences in understanding between supervisor and supervisee; the influence of 'sameness' in ethnicity, race, gender or age may lead to assumptions and collusion between the supervisor and supervisee. Beyond the immediate relationship between PE and the student, it is also important to consider the place that factors such as institutional racism may play and the effect that this can have on both PE (and the power inherent in that role and identity) and student. Kennedy (2013) discusses this in relation to a particular placement situation involving a Black African female student and a white female PE and tutor, where she considers the factors involved in the communication, relationships and interactions during the placement.

As a PE you will need to acknowledge the power differentials within supervision and the PE/student relationship and invite a discussion of them early within the placement, and certainly when discussing the Supervision Contract. This will involve being explicit about the manner in which your power and authority will be used – for example, what is 'negotiable' within the supervisory relationship and what is not?; what will inform your assessment of the student and how this process will be managed (see Chapter 6 on Assessment)? The values for PEs and supervisors within the PEPS (2013b) offers guidance which focuses on the implications of social work values in relation to the assessment process, but can also be helpful as guidance when considering the impact and implications of power and authority within the supervisory relationship. The learning outcome B:10, required to achieve Stage 2 of the PEPS (2013b), specifically requires PEs at Stage 2 to recognise the power dynamics between the PE and the learner.

To practise in the role with anti-oppressive values at the heart, you will need to maintain a continued awareness of the impact of structural oppression and power differentials and demonstrate a willingness to listen, to respond to feedback from the student, to collaborate, and to ensure the relationship is underpinned by openness and honesty.

Supervision and the development of professional practice – for the Practice Educator

So far, this chapter has considered the role that supervision plays within the placement and the key role it has in developing and facilitating student learning and reflection and the role that the PE plays within this. However, providing supervision is often a new role for a PE and is one that needs to be supported and developed as part of the PE's own professional development. Just as this chapter has discussed the importance of ensuring that 'managerial supervision' is integrated with 'reflective supervision' with students, so PEs are also entitled to the same with their supervisors – that is, their supervision should not solely be about analysis and decision making in relation to casework but should also include discussion of the PE's professional development needs and the support and further training they require in this role. There is a specific reference to this in the SWRB *Standards for Employers and Supervision Framework* (SWRB, undated) which states that employers should provide opportunities for CPD and particularly *ensure that PEs are able to contribute to the learning, support and supervision and assessment of students on qualifying and CPD programmes*. PEs are thus aided in discussing their role as PEs and their ongoing development needs during their own professional supervision and by so doing will also be ensuring that the link between effective supervision – their supervision with their student and their own professional supervision – and positive outcomes for service users, is enhanced.

Conclusion

This chapter has looked at the role of the PE in providing effective supervision for safe practice of student social workers. Different models of supervision have been suggested and both the supervisory cycle (within supervision) and the structure of supervision throughout the placement have been examined. The skills, questioning techniques and prompts that a PE can use during supervision to enable student learning have been noted. Issues of power differentials within supervision have been discussed and the necessity for PEs to embrace a continuing awareness of the impact of these differentials within supervision. For many social work students, the supervision offered by the PE will be their first experience of professional supervision, and ensuring that supervision is collaborative and effective can lay important foundations for good practice when qualified. Finally, while the role of supervision in developing the professional practice of the student is paramount, it is also the case that, for PEs, supervision also has an important role to play – as the following quote from Ford and Jones (1987) illustrates: *The supervisory role can be seen as a final stage in the development of the professional role – that of learning to teach the art that one has acquired oneself* (p. 8).

What does the research say?

The significance of the relationship between the PE and the student has previously been noted (see Chapter 3 – 'What does the research say?' and the discussion of Lefevre, 2009 study) and supervision is a key location and conduit for this relationship. Yet as Doel (2010) has noted, there is very little research into the 'fine detail' of what goes on in supervision. However, a small-scale study carried out by Ian Brodie and Val Williams (2012) looks at this.

Brodie and Williams study

- » *Sample* – 16 participants (eight PEs and eight students). The students were undertaking their first placement of 65 days; the PEs were of differing levels of experience and included 'on site' and 'off site' PEs; the students were all undertaking a two-year postgraduate social work programme.

- » *Data collection* – eight supervision sessions involving PEs and students were audio recorded; each student and PE (16) were interviewed.

Key messages highlighted in the research

- » *Perspectives on the supervisory relationship* – both students and PEs valued 'honesty', 'openness', 'reliability' and a 'transparent relationship'. The authors noted that, beyond this consensus, PEs gave greater emphasis to the wider context of the relationship, referring to their role in ensuring accountability and their role in assessment of the student's performance.

- » *Topic coverage in supervision* – this was recorded as a percentage coverage in all recorded sessions as follows.

Topic	% coverage
Academic work (students' academic assignments and portfolio)	13
Administration/practical arrangements (making, checking, confirming meetings and other practical arrangements)	2
Agenda setting (setting and agreeing agendas for supervision)	1
Placement review (reviewing progress of placement, including student learning)	23
Practice discussion (discussing aspects of the student's own practice)	57
Workload checking (reviewing student workload)	3

» The authors suggest that the 'balance' between academic and practice issues, which PEs claimed to provide and students wanted, was in evidence.

» *Activities of PEs and students within supervision* – the authors coded activities of PEs and students during the recorded sessions and interviews and noted the most frequent activities. The top ten activities included the following (in order of those noted most frequently).

1. *Exploring* – PEs used 'exploring' and open ended questions to encourage students to expand and analyse their practice – eg '*how might you go about that?*' The authors report a positive correlation between PE 'exploring' and students engaging in the analysis of a case or practice situation.

2. *Expressing opinion* – PEs provided an opinion on a particular topic or issue. This was highly valued by students – all of the students in interview mentioned the importance to them of accessing the PEs experience and expertise during supervision.

3. *Giving feedback* – significant use of this was made during the supervision session, either the PE providing detailed feedback on an observation or summarising the student's progress over the course of the placement.

4. *Referring to theory* – all students indicated that this was an aspect covered by their PEs within supervision; the taped sessions indicated that this was in the form of direct teaching but that *more typical was the placing of responsibility by the Practice Teacher on to the student to identify and apply theory* (p. 14). PEs made use of a range of learning tools, techniques and activities, such as direct observation, in order to promote student learning.

Concluding, the authors feel that, although based on a small sample, the evidence suggests that the student learning will be enhanced if the following are in place.

» A supervisory relationship that is open and honest.

» Supervision is regular in frequency and balanced in content.

» A practice teacher who is able to explain and explore the application of theory to practice.

» A practice teacher who can offer constructive, specific feedback on student progress and performance.

» A supervisory forum where the student is given an active role in identifying and developing their learning.

Taking it further

Ford, K. and Jones, A. (1987) *Student Supervision*, London: Macmillan – still a very helpful and comprehensive text offering guidance on the differing elements of a student placement.

McKitterick, B. (2012) *Supervision*, Berkshire: Open University Press – this text covers the fundamentals of supervision and may be particularly helpful for social workers who are PEs and/or mentors or supervisors of others. Chapter 5, 'When things go wrong', may also be helpful for PEs who do not feel they are being fully supported or developed in their role as a PE through their own supervision.

Wonnacott, J. (2012) *Mastering Social Work Supervision*, London: Jessica Kingsley – a text written for social work supervisors but which also explains well the link between effective supervision and effective outcomes for service users. This book also refers to the 4x4x4 Model referred to in this chapter. The author, Jane Wonnacott, is also the co-author (with Tony Morrison) of the CWDC (2009) guide for supervisors referred to below.

CWDC (2009) *NQSW: guide for supervisors: newly qualified social worker pilot programme 2009–2010.* Online, available at: dera.ioe.ac.uk/id/eprint/11248 [accessed 5 January 2014] – a freely available resource, written for supervisors of NQSWs within children's services, but which offers a detailed outline of the 4X4X4 Model of Supervision and also has a helpful appendix – Appendix 3 – suggesting 'Questions around the supervisory cycle'.

Brown, A. and Bourne, I. (1996) *The Social Work Supervisor*, Buckingham: Open University Press – Chapter 3 looks particularly at supervision and power.

Lindsay, T. (2003) *An Investigation of Group Learning on Practice Placements*, SWAP report – a report exploring the benefits and good practice guidelines for group supervision of social work students. Online, available at: www.swap.ac.uk/docs/projects/group%20learning%20on%20practice%20placements.pdf [accessed 5 January 2014].

Chapter 6 | Assessment

The material in this chapter links to the following PEPS domains and values statements for PEs and supervisors:

Learning outcome domains required for Stage 1 and Stage 2 PEs

A:3; A:4; B:2; B:6; B:7; all of Domain C

Additional learning outcome domains required for Stage 2 PEs

D:2; D:3; D:6; D:7

Values for PEs and supervisors: 1–7

Chapter aims

- » To establish core principles of fair assessment.
- » To explore the notion of holistic assessment in the context of practice learning.
- » To explore skills, methods and tools to support assessment.

Critical **questions**

1. How do I maintain the role of assessor and supporter of the student – thus ensuring that I assess *in a manner that does not stigmatise or disadvantage individuals and ensures equality of opportunity* (PEPS 2013b, Values Statement 5)?

2. How do I ensure that holistic assessment decisions are the outcomes of informed, evidence-based judgements (Domain C:1 – PEPS, TCSW, 2013b, p 9)?

3. How do I maintain the balance between my own judgement and standardised professional standards?

Introduction

Assessment of a student is a complex activity undertaken in the context of a profession in flux and social work and social care structures undergoing huge changes. The responsibility placed on PEs by the assessment role can be extremely anxiety-provoking, requiring them to make a judgement about a student as to suitability and capability for their own profession. Alongside the accepted demands of this role, PEs are now being asked to carry out assessment in line with new guidelines for 'holistic assessment' using criteria defined within the PCF, which represents a significant shift from the established framework of the NOS that pertained from 2003 until 2012.

We are conscious therefore of the need to assist more experienced PEs to move from the previous competency-based model to the new framework, as well as helping newer PEs to develop relevant skills and knowledge to assess in line with this framework.

The intention of this chapter is to guide the reader to an understanding of what holistic assessment means in practice and how it sits within the broader framework of well-established core principles of effective and fair assessment. The chapter will begin with a brief outline of the background to the introduction of holistic assessment, along with an examination of the terms 'competence' and 'capability'. This will be followed by an exploration of the purpose, process and methods of assessment in practice learning with a focus on the skills required by PEs to meet the PEPS (TCSW, 2013b). The implications of holistic assessment will be looked at within this context. There will be specific discussion about the role and involvement of service users and carers in the assessment of students. Guidance will be given on the assessment of students' written academic and portfolio work and the chapter will conclude with a section on writing a final report.

Rationale for holistic assessment – background and context

The NOS (TOPPS England, 2002a) will be familiar to current PEs and graduates of the social work degree (established in 2003). They were written to define the social work role, values, tasks, and underpinning approaches via core competences in the form of six key roles, further broken down into 21 units and component elements. The standards were also developed as criteria for assessment of students on placement. The process of assessment of competence in practice was characterised by students producing evidence for each unit, allowing PEs to make an overall judgement of competence. At its most simplistic, if all 21 units were evidenced the student was competent. This was complemented by the use of the Code of Practice (GSCC, 2002) to assess the student's understanding of social work values, ethics and professional conduct. The PE's role at final review point was to comment and elaborate on the evidence provided and make a concluding judgement of competence.

This approach was increasingly critiqued. The author can remember many occasions sitting on Practice Assessment Panels with PEs and academic staff feeling uncertain that a student was professionally competent – despite having 'met all the units'.

The conceptual framework of the NOS is based on elements or competencies, each one of which must be evidenced. This can create 'gaps' through which the assessment can fall, since judgements about overall capability may get lost where there is a micro focus on competence.

(TCSW, 2012a, p. 4).

Competence or capability?

Lawson (2013) summarises criticisms of the NOS as a framework for assessment, and in so doing indicates one of the key reasons for the move from 'competence' to 'capability': *Measuring students' work against ... performance indicators, it was argued, failed to capture the full extent of what it meant to be an emotionally intelligent, intellectually astute, ethically aware reflective practitioner.*

The decision to ascribe the word 'capability' to the domains within the PCF, and to introduce it as an alternative to 'competence', helps us think differently in a subtle way about the PE role as assessor. Dictionary definitions will sometimes give capability and competence as synonyms; however the *Oxford English Dictionary* additionally defines capability as *the power or ability to do something*: (*OED*, online). Competence, on the other hand, is defined as *the ability to do something successfully or efficiently* (*OED*, online).

Professional **development prompt**

> » What do the two terms 'capability' and 'competence' mean to you? How might your approach to assessing competence differ from that of assessing capability?

Your thinking may lead you to conclude that in order to assess *competence* you need to see evidence of a completed task, whereas assessing *capability* (the potential to do something) requires more knowledge about the learner, their skill base and, crucially, their thinking. The Social Work Reform Board (DfE, 2010 p. 9) defined capability as: *An integration of knowledge, skills, personal qualities and understanding used appropriately and effectively – not just in familiar and highly focused specialised contexts but in response to new and changing circumstances.* This definition implies the need for skills of reflection, applying evidence-informed knowledge, and a commitment to life-long learning and development (Lawson, 2013).

Williams and Rutter (2010), in considering the difference between professional competence and professional capability, make the point that the Social Work Degree (DoH, 2002) was underpinned by a benchmark statement emphasising the need for skills such as critical thinking and problem-solving to be developed in the practice arena as well as in the academic setting (QAAHE, 2008). Despite this intention, critics of the NOS argue that they skewed assessment toward *describing* rather than *evidencing understanding* of social work activity. This can provide a helpful pointer to the difference; capability implies the ability within students and practitioners to understand the task or intervention in order to be able to contextualise and apply the component elements in other situations. In other words focus must shift from the *outcome* to the *process* of practice and learning. This means, among other skills, being able to apply academic learning in practice. In response to this the Social Work Reform Board developed and made more explicit the need to look at 'bridging the gap' between university and practice by involving practitioners and service users much more in the delivery of the curriculum. The PCF with its developmental and progressive approach to learning and development, from admission to university through to a clear framework for an ASYE, has gone some way towards addressing the deficits of the previous model.

Holistic assessment

Principles for holistic assessment are set out in TCSW (2012m) document *Understanding what is meant by holistic assessment.* These will be referenced throughout the rest of this chapter as an aid to developing robust assessment skills as PEs move to the new framework. The move to the notion of 'holistic assessment' replaces a competency model with a requirement for an assessor to provide an overarching assessment *of the integrated action, not of the performance of each part* (Biggs, 2007, cited in TCSW 2012m). Furthermore, the same document advises that: *There should be a better balance between the evidence presented by students and the professional judgement of practice educators* (TCSW, 2012m). It is important to note that the development of the

PEPS (TCSW 2013b) and the expectation for PEs to be trained and continually professionally develop is central to the development of a model of learning that is intended to integrate aspects of learning and embody an approach based on capability rather than competence. PEs will be key in modelling, facilitating and assessing learning in a manner that it is hoped will support social work practice in becoming more effective, as a direct result of the changes that have been introduced in social work education and beyond into practice.

In order to feel confident in carrying out a holistic assessment it is important for educators to be incorporating into their practice established principles of fair assessment. The next section will review these principles with a view to enabling PEs to underpin their final assessment of a student with a process that is *'trustworthy, reliable and transparent'* (TCSW 2012m).

Effective assessment

Domain C:2, C:3 and C:4 (PEPS, TCSW, 2013b, p 9) makes clear that effective assessment is demonstrated through a clear strategy and using evidence that is robust according to agreed standards.

The component strategic stages of assessment are generally referred to as *planning, collecting* and *weighing* evidence (Cree and Macaulay, 2000; Williams and Rutter, 2010). In order to examine these stages more closely we have chosen to frame them in terms of the questions Why, What and How.

Purpose of assessment – why are you assessing?

Evans (1999, p. 181) describes assessment in the context of social work education as having two broad purposes; to aid students' learning and to ensure standards of entry into the social work profession. These two functions embody the fundamental duality of the role of a PE – that of supporting learning and assessing competence or capability. In our experience the conflict this dual role can create is one of the major anxieties experienced by PEs, and links to the 'critical questions' posed at the beginning of the chapter.

Diagnostic, formative and summative assessment

Beverley and Worsley (2007, p. 129) discuss the conflict that can arise from the dual role of the PE, and point out the necessity for clarity for the student about the purpose of the assessment taking place at any stage of the learning process. Explicitly incorporating the notion of diagnostic, formative and summative assessment into practice learning may help avoid confusion and anxiety for a student and help define and develop the PE's roles of support, education and assessment. Diagnostic assessment is intended to identify learning needs and the types of teaching and learning strategies needed to meet the learner's style (Beverley and Worsley 2007, p. 129). Formative assessment is intended to enable the learner to assimilate feedback in order to progress their learning. Formative feedback may operate both to improve the learning of individual students and to improve the teaching itself (Biggs 2007, p. 164). Summative assessment constitutes the final decision of 'Pass' or 'Fail', normally according to some external criteria.

In order to maximise the value of diagnostic and formative assessment it is important to plan and create opportunities to enable the student to learn from feedback and follow up on subsequent learning needs.

Case **example**

An initial discussion at the Practice Learning Agreement meeting for a first placement in an organisation offering support for carers identified that the student (Sophia) had no previous experience of carrying out an Initial Assessment. This was highlighted as one of the learning opportunities to be offered. In supervision an analysis of skills and knowledge needed for the task was devised by Sophia and the PE with a list of areas where Sophia needed to develop her practice in order to offer an effective intervention (diagnostic stage). Relevant research, teaching and rehearsal then took place to review transferable skills or knowledge already possessed by Sophia, and to address gaps. A direct observation was planned as a formative assessment of the student's learning. It was observed as a result that Sophia did not have enough knowledge of eligibility criteria for the Respite Service so she was asked to research these criteria and present them in the next supervision session. A further discussion confirmed that this knowledge was embedded and this piece of work could then contribute to the summative assessment of Sophia's capability across several PCF domains.

As PE if you followed the steps above you would be meeting Domain C:8, C:9 and C:10 (PEPS, TCSW, 2013b).

The mid-point review

Given the emphasis on progressive and developmental assessment, the mid-point review process can be seen as a vital tool for the review of the student's progress and planning for the second half of placement. This is another opportunity for the student to contribute actively to their learning and assessment, and a key point at which to formally review any self-assessment or diagnostic tools you may have been using.

The subject of assessment – what are you assessing?

Closely allied to the purpose of your assessment is the subject of your assessment. As part of academic learning at university, students are familiar with the notion of learning outcomes and objectives and with the alignment of teaching and assessment methods with learning outcomes. Practice learning should be no different; students should have a clear set of objectives to meet. Assessment should be clearly focused on those objectives and a learning plan and appropriate support and teaching should be provided that takes into account both specific objectives and student learning needs and style. Chapter 4 on 'Enabling learning' discusses the use of a Practice Learning Curriculum, exploring further how objectives can be agreed and met, with an additional section on what the student should 'know about' and 'know how to'.

The question 'what are you assessing?' was ostensibly easier to answer when PEs and students were working with National Occupational Standards which translated into criteria applicable to most social work or social care settings. Although this was a helpful framework, the need to provide evidence against a set of competences meant that on occasion tasks or opportunities had to be manufactured to make sure all required competences were met. The emphasis on evidence sometimes diminished or replaced the process of reflection or discussion by which the PE could have satisfied themselves that the student possessed the requisite skills and knowledge (capability).

The difference now should be that PEs can use learning opportunities that arise naturally from the placement setting and assess performance to make a holistic judgement, using PCF domains to assist in critically analysing *why* a particular intervention was of a satisfactory nature or not, thus informing a more general judgement of whether the student understands a function they are performing and could carry it out under different circumstances or in another context.

The PCF promotes a progressive approach, inviting the PE to make explicit the student's progress throughout placement, and helping the student to understand their development in the context of their overall education and career pathway. All elements of the assessment should contribute to the summative assessment, including areas of relative weakness or uncertain development. As stated, the process of the placement should become more important than the outcome.

It is therefore essential for both students and PEs to be familiar with the PCF and to be aware of the level required of the student by the end of the placement. As a PE you may find it helpful to seek and promote agreement about how work carried out in your agency relates to the appropriate level of the PCF. It is vital that every member of the assessment team *and* the student understand and take a consistent approach to the assessment framework.

Professional **development prompt**

Write down the functions of your agency and the component daily tasks and roles undertaken by workers in your service (it may be helpful to do this over the course of one day). Map them to the PCF and try to ensure you are working with the appropriate level. Discuss with other PEs in your team or service and try to establish consistency and agreement around how the domains of the PCF could be applied to any of these tasks or functions. Bearing in mind the norms of your agency, think about how a student could demonstrate capability (levels of skill, areas of knowledge, behaviour or approach) within the domains. This may range from dress code, or language used when addressing service users, to processes for referral or criteria for closing cases.

Involving the student

One of the fundamental tenets of good practice proposed within this book is that the student should be involved at all stages of the process. All of the professional frameworks now guiding the conduct and performance of social workers place emphasis on the need for social workers and students to take responsibility for their own learning and development. The PCF (Domain 1 – *Professionalism*) emphasises the centrality of supervision and states that by the end of the first placement the student *should recognise and act on own learning needs in response to practice experience* (TCSW, 2012h). The HCPC Standards of Conduct and Ethics (Guide for Students)(7) requires a student to *act within the limits of your knowledge and skills* (7) (HCPC, 2012d).

Williams and Rutter (2010) advocate that the planning and organisation of the assessment process should be a shared process between enabler and learner. Jonathan Parker (2010b) likewise emphasises the importance of involving the student in planning and goes further in setting out suggestions for encouraging the self-assessment of progress. He makes the point that although students may be aware of what is to be assessed and have some sense of the assessment criteria and even of exemplary practice gained through observation and shadowing, their confidence in their ability to achieve certain standards is a crucial factor. He puts forward a model consisting of a self-efficacy questionnaire which can be used diagnostically to identify learning needs and can be reviewed regularly at various milestones throughout the placement.

In addition, the templates and pro-formas used for the assessment of students' practice, such as direct observations, should be designed to enable the student to analyse, reflect and self-evaluate. Involving the student in self-assessment should be a central consideration for PEs, and demonstrating this concern within your practice will help you meet Domain C:7 of PEPS (TCSW, 2013b).

Moreover, Williams and Rutter (2010, p. 103) make the point that the dynamics produced by the assessment element of the PE role is where the power imbalance between student and PE can most obviously manifest itself. The principle therefore of sharing responsibility and enabling students to develop the tools and confidence to self-assess and contribute to the developmental process is a key to maximising the sharing of power.

The process and methods of assessment – how are you assessing?

Collecting evidence

As PE you need to use *all relevant evidence ... from a range of sources ... to produce evidence-based judgments* (Domain C:3; C:6; PEPS TCSW, 2013b p. 9). Given your responsibility as gatekeeper of the profession, you have a duty to *seek* the best possible evidence, just as a student should be seeking to *provide* the best possible evidence. The question is 'what is the best evidence?' The process of collecting evidence should be a continuous, developmental process that enables the student and PE to make links between what they are doing and learning. As indicated earlier in this chapter it is intended that the shift toward holistic assessment and capability statements will prompt PE and student to focus more on the *process* rather than the *outcome* of practice. The questions 'how' and 'why', rather than 'what' should be central to an examination and validation of evidence. One of the central contributions to the debate over the past five years about how social work practice is to be improved has been the insistence that social workers need to develop skills in critical thinking with an ability to think through situations that do not proceed in a linear, predictable fashion; Munro (2011) talks of a move from a compliance culture to a learning culture with an emphasis on capabilities relating to knowledge, critical reflection and analysis. The PCF and the PEPS reflect this. Hence practice learning experiences should encourage the development and demonstration of these skills. This demands of PEs the ability to promote critical thinking and discuss subtlety and complexity in a way that was previously not necessarily inherent in the process of evidencing competence.

This is not to say that concrete evidence should not be sought – more that the student should be required to analyse and explain the thinking behind their work, thus enabling the PE to be satisfied that the student is developing a sense of their professional role, knowledge and value base, and that the required skills are in place. To this end, sources of evidence should continue to include work-based products such as agency records, case notes and reports. However, in addition you need to have regular sight of the student's 'working out'. Inevitably this links back to the centrality of reflective supervision as a forum for learning, dialogue and assessment, as discussed in Chapter 5.

The role of the off-site PE

It is acknowledged that the new holistic approach may present challenges for off-site PEs who may not have intimate knowledge or oversight of the student's daily work.

Indeed they may not have specialist knowledge of the placement setting. It will be particularly important for them therefore to develop ways of ensuring they can maintain oversight of the student's development and the tools developed for demonstrating the student's reflective abilities will be key. See Chapter 7 for a more detailed exploration of how an off-site PE and practice supervisor can work effectively together.

Helping students understand a holistic approach to learning and assessment

It can be argued that one of the key determinants for a successful placement is the openness of a student to learning, entailing reflection on their practice and willingness to respond to feedback. Chapter 8 on Reflective Practice will give you as PE some tools to teach and assess students on this basis. The 'Douglas Model', referred to in Chapter 4, can assist in analysing and diagnosing – even assessing – component requirements for effective practice. Lawson (2013) makes the point that *it is the way the practitioner puts these skills together, integrates them and makes judgements about how to adapt them to different contexts ... that makes the whole.* Holistic assessment requires the PE to analyse performance (identifying strengths and areas needing development) using the PCF domains, but over and above that to make a judgement on how the learner has pulled the capabilities together in a demonstration of *overall* capability. Lawson (2013) puts forward the model of the *doughnut of holistic assessment* to illustrate this approach – nominating the *hole in the middle* as the *reflective space* which allows the PE and student together to make sense of the component parts.

Weighing evidence: achieving a fair and justifiable assessment decision

Perhaps the most testing aspect of the PE role is the summative assessment – making a decision about whether a student is competent (or capable) or not. This can be very stressful for a PE and it must be emphasised again that you should seek support at all stages of the process. Your decision will be conveyed to the University Assessment Board as a final recommendation. It is therefore crucial that you feel able to make a sound judgement.

Fair assessment

As Biggs (2007, p. 184) points out, *critics argue that holistic assessment involves a 'subjective' judgement.* He goes on to debate whether any assessment can be otherwise. This seems a moot point – there is no doubt that even while being required to exercise your professional judgement as to whether a student meets standards required, you need to justify your decision both to the student and to external bodies. The following principles are intended to help you make sure that the evidence upon which you base your decision is rigorous and underpinned by fairness. These are clearly written into PEPS Domain C:4 (TCSW, 2013b).

» *Relevance* – have you chosen an appropriate method of assessment to measure the task or skill being assessed? Report-writing skills can be assessed via a report rather than through discussion, although a discussion may ascertain what learning needs the student has before undertaking a report, and may help to illustrate thinking and decision-making skills.

» *Validity* – is the evidence really demonstrating what it is intended to test? Is it related to an agreed objective or criterion?

» *Reliability* – would the same student be assessed similarly if they repeated the activity more than once? Would a different assessor come to the same conclusion if measuring against the same standards? Does the evidence build a consistent picture?

» *Sufficiency* – have you ensured that the student has had enough opportunities to demonstrate consistency? Are you satisfied they can do so?

» *Authenticity* – is the evidence being assessed the work of the individual being assessed? This can be a particular issue with written academic pieces which can be plagiarised. Also students co-working with colleagues will need to be assessed according to the input they provide to an activity.

Professional **development prompt**

Taking one learning objective from your Learning Agreement with the student apply the above standards to the assessment strategy and write down how you have ensured they apply.

Over and above the standards applied above, is the notion of sensitivity to diversity. This brings into the equation considerations relating to students with particular support needs, which may stem from disability, caring commitments, cultural views and beliefs, race or ethnic background. Within particular chapters (2, 3 and 7) we have offered suggestions as to how to attend to these issues in order that all students may be assessed on a 'level playing field' and to minimise discrimination (see Standard 6, Values for PEs and supervisors, PEPS, TCSW, 2013b p. 11).

Triangulation

One way of ensuring fairness (Beverley and Worsley, 2007) is to introduce and use a variety of assessment methods that will play to the strengths of different students and also allow for the identification of weaker areas of practice. Achievement across the piece is required. Further and more detailed discussion about ensuring students with different backgrounds and needs can be fairly assessed is contained in Chapter 4.

Owing to the inherent difficulty in gaining a standard assessment of social work practice several authors advise triangulation of evidence (Doel and Shardlow, 1996; Evans, 1999; Lawson, 2013). This means offering a range of opportunities and assessment methods and involving several people in the assessment. These can be people with different roles such as colleagues, allied professionals and administrative staff in the agency. Their different perspectives on the same piece of work can inform a rounded assessment of the process and impact of the intervention. A systematic and transparent approach to this is needed, so that the student's development is noted and analysed, the contributions of each participant meaningful, and appropriate feedback and support is given to the student as part of ongoing developmental supervision. TCSW (2012m) offers the criteria for trustworthy judgements outlined by Knight (2006) as another benchmark for fair assessment. These include observations of several slices of practice by different observers with reference to known and agreed criteria or standards. This reminds us of the importance of preparing the team (see Chapter 3) and of the need for all involved to be familiar with the objectives and subject of assessment.

An alternative criterion to apply to your review of your assessment methods is to consider if you have used a full and balanced range of concrete, discursive and feedback evidence. Concrete evidence would refer to work products or other evidence that can be obtained from direct observation, production of certificates, and so on. Discursive evidence is that gained from sources such as discussion, reflective accounts, and supervision. Feedback evidence is that obtained from others such as service users and professional colleagues. This in itself can be in concrete or discursive formats. Evidence of all three types supports the validity of your professional assessment.

Professional **development prompt**

Develop a template that a colleague can use to comment specifically on a student's performance with key objectives and key references to relevant skills, knowledge, or even a relevant PCF level descriptor.

Involvement of the service user/carer

Ensuring effective, meaningful involvement and feedback from service users and carers merits a section of its own. It is a principle now enshrined in the Social Work Reform Board's recommendations for social work education that service users and carers should be involved at all stages of a student's social work education. Further, the reforms include the requirement to establish partnerships composed of HEIs, employers and service users and carers which will work together to design and deliver course provision (TCSW, 2012k).

There are many examples of genuine commitment to working in partnership with service users and carers but it is apparent that, even though placements provide natural opportunities for the participation of service users, their involvement remains inconsistent. Wallcraft *et al.* (2012) conclude that although service user and carer involvement is widespread their involvement is weakest in the area of assessment; good practice is not routinely shared across institutions and some groups are not fully participating; these include children, young people and people with learning disability.

Examples from existing practice within universities include:

> » service users/carers developing and delivering a module or sessions at university;

> » service users/carers leading seminars and marking reflective accounts of sessions;

> » service users/carers participating in role-plays and simulation exercises.

On placement, it would seem that the most common involvement of a service user/ carer in the student's learning is through the traditional feedback form or dialogue at the end of a direct observation. And yet there seems no real reason why some of the ideas above could not be transferred to a placement setting with some planning. For example, the author is aware of one nursing course where during placement a service user is supported and trained appropriately to meet regularly with the student to give feedback on skills and development. This may well be an activity that is feasible for social work placements.

We would suggest that PEs could and should work together with service users/carers within a practice setting to teach and assess students in a meaningful and specific way. It is accepted that working with service users can present challenges for both parties. However solutions can be found to maximise the benefits gained.

> ## Professional **development prompt**
>
> Plan to involve service users/carers in a specific aspect of your student's learning and associated assessment. Think about the benefits and the challenges, and find solutions. Discuss with a service user/carer where possible.

Summary of core principles of assessment

This section of the chapter has discussed principles of assessment which should underpin your work with a student and allow you to undertake a fair assessment. The concept of holistic assessment has been introduced but the emphasis has been on assisting the PE to develop sound assessment skills dependent on the following core principles.

- » Clarity of purpose of assessment – PEPS Domain C:8; C:9.
- » Clarity of planning – assessment being developmental (diagnostic/formative/summative) – PEPS Domain C:2.
- » Clarity and transparency about what is being assessed and what criteria are being applied – PEPS Domain C:1; C:7.
- » The need to involve the student – PEPS Domain C:7; C:8; C:9.
- » Basing your decision on a range of evidence – triangulation – PEPS Domain C:6.
- » Ensuring evidence is relevant, valid, reliable, sufficient, authentic – PEPS Domain C:4.

Direct observation of practice

Traditionally seen as the most reliable way of gathering evidence of a student's practice, direct observations have been retained in the guidance on assessment of a student's practice (TCSW, 2013b). Indeed, within the PEPS, Domain C:5 makes this form of assessment a particular requirement.

Direct observation remains one of the most anxiety-provoking activities for a student. Inevitably the artificiality of the situation along with the discomfort that can be aroused for both student and service user can impact considerably on the performance of the student, and careful planning, implementation and feedback are necessary to maximise the learning that can take place. Creative ideas such as using one direct observation as a diagnostic or formative learning and assessment activity early in placement can help to remove some of the anxiety from the process.

Core principles for making direct observation a safe and effective method of assessment have long been established (Williams and Rutter, 2010; Koprowska, 1999). The authors' training of PEs has drawn upon the University of York Model (Koprowska, 1999) in its use of three stages – before, during and after the observation. Translated into planning, activity and feedback, the student's participation is to be encouraged throughout, with the use of discussion, templates and pro-formas that assist reflection and evaluation.

In order to use direct observations in a way that will enable holistic assessment, we would suggest that in addition to clear planning of objectives and analysis of outcomes, emphasis could usefully be placed upon the critical reflection skills which enable a student to analyse their intervention, evaluate it, explain their thinking and understanding, and link it to their development and future learning. If this is to be the case then the skill of the PE lies in creating a safe environment in which the student can explore and test their ideas and take responsibility for the intervention that has occurred. The student should be enabled to reflect on the service user's participation in the event in a way that demonstrates empathy alongside the use of theory and research to understand and explain their intervention and the wider contexts of their lives. In order to maximise the learning from an observation the PE may wish to review good practice principles of using feedback (further explored in Chapter 4) and employ models that encourage critical reflection and analysis (see Chapter 8).

> ## Professional **development prompt**
>
> Think about how you can create a safe environment for a student and service user for a direct observation.

Assessing or marking academic work

As a PE you may be required to contribute to the assessment of the student's portfolio work, such as case studies or reflective accounts. Some universities may invite you to grade a piece of written work; others may require you at least to validate the practice described within. All will expect you to verify, validate and evaluate the contents of a student portfolio. If you are applying for Stage 2 you will need to demonstrate the ability to mark learners' academic or assessed work (Domain C:15). If this is not within your remit you may satisfy this requirement by commenting or contributing in the way described below.

The following points are intended to help you in assessing a student's work (taken from Tim Ward (2002) *A Toolkit for Practice Teachers*).

» Be clear from the programme and tutor how far you can advise the student.

» Refer to the *Practice Learning Handbook* for criteria as to academic marking of pieces.

» Read it through quickly to get a gut reaction as to whether it is good, bad or marginal.

» Read it through more slowly using the criteria. All criteria will need to have been met.

» Note down strengths and weaknesses, perhaps under criteria headings; if there are more strengths than weaknesses then a pass is generally indicated.

» Feedback should provide an overall statement about the quality of the work followed by more specific comments. Try to balance negatives with positives.

» When feeding back use language and concepts contained within the guidance for the piece and any academic marking criteria you are using.

» Where a piece of work has failed you need to be very specific about what parts have failed and why.

Commenting on the student's academic work

Most work to be submitted in a placement portfolio is not given an academic mark. However, PEs will play a pivotal role in helping the student choose appropriate pieces of work to present as evidence, validating the student's practice and ensuring it conforms to agency procedures. If you are working towards assessing a student in a holistic fashion, involving understanding a student's thinking, it is vital that you both enable them to create good quality written pieces of reflective work and assess its value in demonstrating their developing capability.

Writing the final report as part of a holistic assessment (link to 'Critical question 1')

The culmination of the assessment process for a PE is the writing of a final report which reflects the student's development and achievements throughout the placement and complements the student's contributions to the portfolio. It is essential to ensure that your final assessments are informed by evidence (PEPS Domain C3, C6, C10 (TCSW, 2013b); TCSW, 2012a). Under a competency model PEs have been accustomed to validating and supplementing evidence provided by a student and agreeing a 'Pass' if the student had evidenced all standards sufficiently. The holistic assessment process requires a rather different emphasis. TCSW (2012a) suggests an assessment report

provides an overall judgement, taking into account capability across all nine domains of the PCF ... This may be followed by an assessment comment on each of the nine domains identifying strengths and areas for development/concern (including reference to individual capability statements where there are areas of concern).

It can be seen from this excerpt that the process has almost been reversed; in contrast to a position where the component parts (NOS) were considered in isolation, and if met satisfactorily led to a 'Pass' conclusion, a holistic assessment requires an overall judgement based on the professional experience of the assessor, with a 'Pass' decision being informed to a greater or lesser degree by the component parts (Capability Statements).

Making your decision

Lawson (2013), when discussing the change in language from competence to capability, offers the analogy of the *lens of a camera shifting from close-up to wide-angle*, arguing that if *capability encourages us to be mindful of 'the whole' as well as the individual parts ... then ... holistic assessment goes hand in hand with a capability framework.* This can allow for weighting within component elements, and crucially allows for weaknesses and areas for development to be identified without necessarily leading to a 'Fail'.

Where learning or performance objectives are complex, the judgement of the assessor is considered central in making a holistic decision about the quality of performance.

(Biggs, 2007, cited in TCSW, 2012a, p. 5)

It can be seen from this that a holistic assessment decision is in no way a purely subjective decision but in fact the summation of a full understanding of the complex activity of social work within its local and social context.

To understand and undertake a holistic approach to assessment, the partial and the contextual must be considered together. In this way, we arrive at a synthesis of specific and general, discrete and dynamic. This is a truly holistic approach to assessment.

(Doel *et al.*, 2002, p. 39)

Principles for writing a final report

These principles act as a summary of good practice as reflected throughout the book – the final report should present no surprises, and should embody the flow from initial Practice Learning Agreement through mid-point review, forming a staging post before a student moves on to the next level of learning or practice. The student should contribute their own perspective and share ownership of the report's conclusions.

» There should be a clear agreement with the student about the report-writing process; for example, sources of evidence, use of feedback from colleagues/service users.

» The process of gathering evidence starts at the beginning of the placement and continues throughout.

» Accessible records should be kept of any evidence you propose to use, for example supervision notes.

» Supervision is key to the process of developing a student's thinking and self-evaluation skills.

» Using a variety of evidence sources promotes fairness in any assessment.

» The evidence should support the recommendation made or concerns outlined – using the appropriate level of the PCF.

» Evidence should be relevant, valid, sufficient and authentic.

» Developmental needs should be identified and made clear, linked to the PCF – this is a crucial part of the student's personal and professional development planning.

» There should be a clear recommendation as to whether the student should pass or fail practice.

» The student and tutor should have an accurate signed record of the report.

Conclusion

This chapter has reviewed key principles in establishing a fair assessment process. This has been taken further by reference to holistic assessment, and the importance of underpinning holistic assessment with core principles of sound assessment has been noted. Particular tools and methods have been explored in relation to enabling a student's critical thinking, an essential indicator for a PE in assessing capability. The involvement of service users and carers in practice learning has been considered and PEs invited to develop their own practice in line with PEPS in order to promote and model effective practice.

Taking it further

TCSW is responsible through its endorsement process for ensuring universities and employers work together to implement the PEPS (2013b) and for ensuring that the PCF is used in the learning and development of social workers throughout their education and career, including as a basis for assessment. In addition to these frameworks, a move to holistic assessment, again throughout education and beyond, has been implemented. TCSW has published a number of helpful guidance documents on its Website; this chapter has referred to the following in some detail:

» PEPS (2013b);

» understanding what is meant by holistic assessment (TCSW 2012m);

» assessing practice using PCF guidance (TCSW 2012a).

In addition, Hilary Lawson (2013) has published a helpful guide: *Guide to the Professional Capability Framework and the Assessed and Supported Year in Employment*, available at Community Care Inform. This offers the reader a practical view of how holistic assessment can work in practice alongside the PCF.

The material in this chapter links to the following PEPS domains and values statements for PEs and supervisors:

Learning outcome domains required for Stage 1 and Stage 2 PEs

A:1; A:2; A:3; A:4; A:5; A:7; B:2; B:3; B:4; B:5; B:7; B:8; C:2; C:3; C:4; C:5; C:6; C:7; C:8; C:9; C:10; C:11; C:14; C:16

Additional learning outcome domains required for Stage 2 PEs

B:10; D:3; D:5; D:7

Values for PEs and supervisors: 1, 3, 4, 5, 6

Chapter aims

- » To consider the range of difficulties that may arise during a practice placement, and the role of the PE in managing these situations.

- » To explore the processes and procedures to be followed in difficult practice situations (including working with 'marginal' and 'failing' students).

- » To explore a range of tools, methods and approaches that the PE can use to assist them in such situations.

Critical **questions**

- » What is the appropriate balance between support and assessment within my PE role?

- » What is the limit of my accountability as compared with that of the university?

- » How much leeway do I give to a student with specific needs?

Introduction

In most cases, the practice placement will progress smoothly; the student will be enthusiastic and motivated to learn and will demonstrate a developing level of skills, knowledge and underpinning values throughout the course of placement. As a PE you are most likely to find that your summative assessment of the student will result in a 'Pass' recommendation at the end of the assessment period. The likelihood of you supervising a placement that ends in the making of a 'Fail' recommendation is probably less than 5 per cent (Wilson *et al.*, 2008).

However, during any individual student's period of practice learning, you may encounter either a short, or possibly a slightly more extended period, where some degree of difficulty arises. Difficulties can arise in respect of the learning opportunities, management, support, teaching or assessment aspects of the placement or due to some degree of concern about the rate of progress or degree of learning being achieved by the student. However, the vast majority of difficulties can be successfully addressed and overcome. Early recognition and an open, shared discussion of the problem, leading on to prompt implementation of an action plan or strategy to deal with the problem, is often the key. Adopting a strategy of delay in dealing with an issue of concern in the hope that that any problem will eventually resolve itself is, however, rarely a successful strategy.

The Practice Learning System: practice placements

While any discussion of 'difficulties' in respect of social work student practice placements is often regarded as synonymous with a student 'failing' or struggling to achieve an adequate standard of professional practice, as a PE you also need to be aware of the whole range of other difficulties or problems that can arise within the placement learning system during a placement. You need to additionally understand what your role and responsibilities as a PE are within the overall Practice Learning System (see diagram) when difficulties arise. This chapter will therefore begin by looking at some of the areas of difficulty that most commonly arise on placements. Later sections of the chapter will then focus more specifically on working with 'marginal' or 'failing' social work students.

The Practice Learning System: practice placements

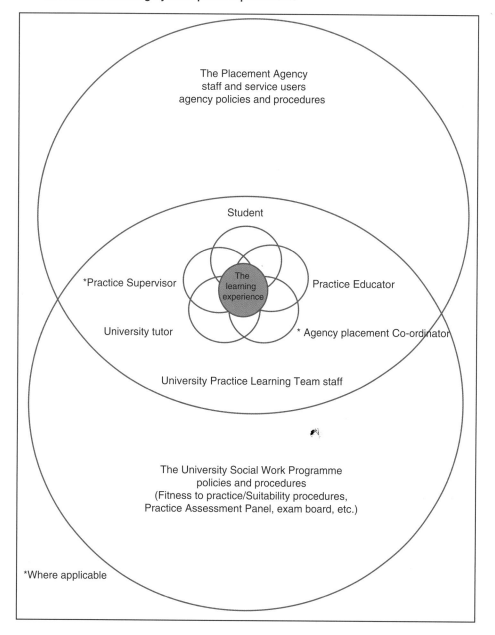

The Placement Agency
staff and service users
agency policies and procedures

Student

*Practice Supervisor

The learning experience

Practice Educator

University tutor

* Agency placement Co-ordinator

University Practice Learning Team staff

The University Social Work Programme
policies and procedures
(Fitness to practice/Suitability procedures,
Practice Assessment Panel, exam board, etc.)

*Where applicable

As the Practice Learning System diagram illustrates, the student and PE work together in a collaborative learning partnership that is located within a much larger learning system, encompassing the placement agency and the university processes, policies and procedures.

Within this learning system a range of other professionals are also employed (such as the university tutor) to support the placement and the learning experience of the student. A Practice Supervisor (PS) may also be allocated for some, but not all, placements. A PS is a placement agency member of staff who offers on-site supervision, casework management, accountability and support to social work students where there is an off-site PE in place. Further information about the roles and responsibilities of PSs and off-site PEs can be found in Appendix 3.

In larger organisations a staff member (usually a member of the agency's workforce development team, known as a practice learning or placement co-ordinator) will co-ordinate, advise and support all practice placements, PEs and PSs within their own organisation, sometimes offering support groups and training sessions for PEs in addition to more individual support and advice. In other social care organisations there may be no placement agency co-ordinator role. In these circumstances the university's Practice Learning Team, university tutor, placement agency colleagues or the PE's own line manager may be the key individuals that can potentially offer support to the PE when dealing with difficulties on placement. Some universities also offer regular training and support groups for PEs and PSs.

Hughes (2006, cited in Maclean and Lloyd, 2008) uses the concept of an orchestra to represent both the number and range of individuals and roles collaboratively involved in the placement. Hughes likens the role of the PE to that of the conductor of the orchestra, as it is the PE's job to manage and co-ordinate the input of all those involved in the placement.

As outlined in Chapter 3 it is therefore important as a PE to prepare for this 'conductor' or management aspect of your role, at the start of each placement. Part of your preparation will involve knowing what the university course requirements are. If you are an on-site PE, you will already be familiar with your own agency's work, policies and procedures. However, if working as an off-site PE, you will additionally need to give thought to how you will familiarise yourself with the work of the placement agency, liaise with the on-site PS and develop a positive working relationship with them, as well as with the student. Time invested in good preparation; building positive working relationships; clarifying roles and expectations with all parties before placement in the Practice Learning Agreement meeting and through the drawing up of a Supervision Agreement; collaboration and shared dialogue in the early stages of placement can often prevent problems arising. Directly undertaking this co-ordinating role in respect of a placement would enable you to meet most of PEPS Domain A:5. Knowing where you can seek support for yourself as a PE if difficulties arise on placement should also form part of your own preparation and planning for placement. This is discussed in Chapter 9.

Professional **development prompt**

Think about the Practice Learning System (see diagram) from your own perspective as a PE.

Who are the key individuals that you could access for advice, guidance or support when dealing with any potential difficulties on placement, and how would you make contact with them?

What type of support might you need from different individuals? (For example, information about implementation of placement or placement agency procedures, emotional or supervisory support, workload relief or someone to discuss your assessment of student progress with.)

What existing or new networks of support might you be able to access, if difficulties arise?

Thinking about and then applying the above issues will contribute towards meeting PEPS Domains D:3, D:5 and D:7.

What kind of placement difficulties may arise?

Most PEs express anxiety around having to deal with difficulties relating to a student's poor practice or having to assess a student as 'failing' or 'marginal'. However, any exploration of placement difficulties needs to start by considering 'difficulties' within the broader framework of the whole Practice Learning System. This means placing the student at the centre of the picture and considering what range of placement difficulties can arise for the student themselves in practice placements that may impede or negatively impact on their learning, as well as considering issues of student capability. The degree of emphasis given to the educative, management, assessment and support functions of the PE role over the course of the placement will depend on the type of placement difficulty that occurs; the level of the placement (first or final); and the particular point in the placement that the difficulty arises.

Common placement difficulties

» Difficulty in obtaining a particular type of learning opportunity that the student requires to be able to adequately demonstrate evidence of a particular aspect of their practice skills or to help them develop baseline knowledge of their role within the placement (Dove and Skinner, 2010).

» A significant period of sickness or workplace absence of the student, PE or an unforeseen change of PS or PE mid-placement (Furness and Gilligan, 2004).

» A period of agency crisis in terms of incoming work, organisational or staff changes within the workplace (Furness and Gilligan, 2004) may mean that the student's needs get temporarily overlooked, resulting in opportunities for either informal or formal supervision or a more detailed oversight of the student's practice being reduced for a period of time.

» A delay in obtaining access to the agency's computer systems (used for case recording and/or e-mail communications with other professionals).

» The health or personal circumstances of the enabler or learner (Bartoli et al., 2008).

» Unhelpful processes in supervision or differences in expectations and perception between the PS, PE and student (Beverley and Worsley, 2007).

» Issues of inappropriate 'matching' between student and placement or in respect of the quality of the placement setting as a suitable practice learning opportunity (Thompson, 2006, Furness and Gilligan, 2004).

» The attitude or motivation of the student (Marsh et al., no date).

» Lack of student experience in relation to the agency function.

» Poor practice performance of the student (Thompson, 2006b).

Concerns regarding 'failing' or 'marginal' students do not usually occur in isolation but often present themselves within the context of a range of other factors (Burgess et al., 1998). The PE therefore needs to be open to discussing and addressing all of the difficulties apparent within the learning system with a view to removing any barriers to student learning that may exist, rather than focusing solely on 'pathologising' the student or 'making the student the problem'.

There is further research available regarding the range of factors that have been found to affect placement learning. These references can be found at the end of the chapter.

Professional **development prompt**

» Think back to a situation where you were a learner or were a social work student on placement. What difficulties (minor or major) did you encounter?

» Were these issues raised with your PE?

» If these issues were raised with your PE, how were they discussed and subsequently addressed or resolved?

» If you did not raise these issues with your PE, why did you feel unable to raise these issues with them?

» Did you raise any issues with your tutor (if applicable)? If so, how were these concerns dealt with?

Authority and power

As has been discussed in Chapters 3, 5 and 6, in your role as PE you need to consider how you will discuss with the student issues around the authority and power invested in the PE role (see the values statement for PEs and supervisors: *identify and question their own values and prejudices, the use of authority and power in the assessment relationship, and recognise and act upon the implications for their assessment practice* (TCSW, 2013b, p. 11).

The Practice Learning Agreement meeting offers an opportunity for the initial introduction of information about what procedures and sources of support are available to the student (and the PE) if disagreements or difficulties arise during the placement (NOPT, 2013). You may alternatively wish to raise the issue of what to do in the event of difficulties, during the process of drawing up a Supervision Agreement with the student (see Chapter 5 on Supervision). If you are an off-site PE, organising a three-way meeting with the student and PS at an early stage of the placement may similarly provide a useful opportunity for a shared discussion of these matters. PEPS Domain C:11 also advises that PEs should *ensure that disagreements about assessment judgements and complaints ... are managed in accordance with agreed procedures* (TCSW, 2012c, p. 8).

It may be useful to consider revisiting Chapter 4 on Enabling Learning to think about the range of approaches you can use as a PE to create a safe learning environment for the student. Addressing this issue in practice will enable you to meet PEPS Domain A:1. It is also important that the student is empowered so that they are able to engage in honest communication with the PE at an early stage of the placement, or as soon as possible, if difficulties become apparent.

> ### Case **example**
>
> One of my own social work student placement experiences involved working in a residential children's home. I had an on-site PE, but rarely received any formal or informal supervision as we were not usually on shift at the same time. I was never left as the sole member of staff on duty, but was regularly used as the second staff member. There were staff shortages throughout the period of the placement and many of the residential workers on duty were agency staff. I received a brief induction on the first day of the placement but thereafter was expected to 'fend for myself'. I did not make any direct complaint to the PE, as I felt any suggestion that this arrangement was unsatisfactory would lead to me be being seen as 'not coping' and negatively impact on my assessment. I also did not think about contacting my university tutor as an alternative source of support, as there were no written guidelines provided by the university regarding student contact with the tutor during the placement. After making it successfully to the end of the placement, I did raise my concerns with my tutor about my placement experience. The university responded positively to my concerns and development work was undertaken with the placement to ensure it would be suitable if used again.

This practice example serves to illustrate the real extent of the power imbalance inherent in the assessment relationship between student and PE, and the degree to which this can become a real barrier to a student, raising concerns about difficulties they encounter on placement with their PE.

Understanding the procedures to be followed when difficulties arise – what do I do?

A range of difficulties can arise over the course of a placement, from a fairly minor issue that can be promptly resolved, to a major issue of concern such as an incident of serious professional misconduct by a student that may result in the immediate suspension and perhaps the subsequent termination of the student's placement.

Each university would normally provide the PE with a *Practice Learning Handbook* at the start of the placement that contains information about the relevant assessment requirements, learning outcomes and procedures for the placement. Most universities will additionally offer online access to documentation relating to the placement and practice learning processes.

While students are expected to work in accordance with the *Guidance on conduct and ethics for students* (HCPC, 2012d), they are not required to register with the HCPC while undertaking their social work training. Any issues to do with professional suitability regarding social work students on placement will therefore be dealt with by the university's own suitability procedures. Thus PEs play a key role in highlighting concerns to universities.

Addressing placement concerns and difficulties

In the first instance, concerns or difficulties should usually be raised by any of the parties involved, directly. The flowchart, 'Addressing Placement Concerns and Difficulties' below, provides an overview of the processes that are generally followed when difficulties arise on placement.

If you (the student, PE, PS or tutor) have a concern in relation to the placement you could use the flowchart below for guidance.

If you (the student, practice educator, practice supervisor or tutor) have a concern in relation to the placement you should:

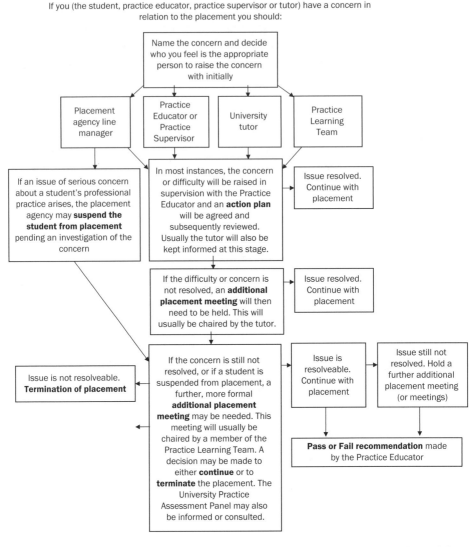

Figure 7.2 Addressing placement concerns and difficulties flowchart. Adapted from the UCLan Practice Learning Handbook, 2012, p. 16). Most universities will have procedures based on similar principles.

Suspension or termination of a placement

Usually, where there are concerns about a student's general rate of progress on placement, or if insufficient learning opportunities are available, the action planning process will be used (see the 'Addressing Placement Concerns and Difficulties Flowchart'). However, if a student's practice is regarded as unsafe, unethical, dangerous or damaging to the degree that if the student were an employee, they would be suspended from work, it may be necessary for the PE or PS to consult immediately with the line manager of the placement agency and for a decision to be taken by the agency to suspend the student prior to any additional placement meeting taking place. In such circumstances the university placement tutor and the relevant member of the university's Practice Learning Team should be immediately informed and the way forward discussed. The placement agency may also need further time to investigate the practice concerns raised before a follow-up placement meeting can be held. If the issue of concern can be dealt with through implementation of an agreed action plan then it is likely that the placement will be able to continue. However, if the issue cannot be satisfactorily resolved the decision may be taken at the additional placement meeting to terminate the placement.

Making a 'Fail' recommendation

The responsibility for making the final decision to fail a student in relation their placement rests with the Exam or Programme Assessment Board of the university. If you make the decision as a PE to make a 'Fail' recommendation, you therefore need to be clear that this is a recommendation rather than final decision (link to 'Critical question 2') and as such your assessment and recommendation can be queried. In rare circumstances your recommendation may even be overturned by the university. However, the university does not often do this, as the PE's professional judgement is trusted. This does depend though, on the PE having justified and evidenced their decision. Within some university programmes, if a student is assessed as 'failing', the university will additionally appoint a second opinion PE to provide an independent assessment of the situation (Maclean and Lloyd, 2008). However, not all universities use a second opinion process, so again it is important to familiarise yourself with the university procedure relevant to each student placement.

Defining the nature of the problem or difficulty

As a PE you need to have a good understanding of the systems and procedures that may need to be followed in a range of practice situations. However, you also need to be able to utilise a range of tools, methods, knowledge and skills to assist you in dealing with the range of varied placement difficulties that can arise.

The term 'difficulty' is defined as a task or problem that is not easy to understand or solve (*Collins English Dictionary*). In order to move forward positively with any given problematic situation on placement, then, it is important for the student, PE and PS (where relevant) to first of all be able to discuss and collaboratively define or agree on the nature of the problem. Once this is achieved you will then be able to draw up a relevant action plan together with the student and other members of the learning partnership, to support the student in solving or resolving these issues.

Professional **development prompt**

After reading through the case example of Joy below, consider:

» What the issues of concern might be?

» How might you prepare for supervision with Joy?

» Referring back to the Practice Learning System diagram, who might you contact?

Case **example**

(Joy is placed in a statutory setting and undertaking her final placement (PLO is an abbreviation of the term, practice learning opportunity).

There was no indication that Joy would struggle with the PLO when she began, but it quickly emerged that Joy was finding the tasks involved in social work difficult. Early in the placement I had asked her to complete a referral form for a family she had met and would be working with. She said she would do it and when I left she burst into tears and ran off. On another occasion Joy said she couldn't take the lead in a home visit as she said she was too afraid, despite having observed many. Then on a direct observation of practice with a service user, on the way home Joy cried as she felt it had gone so badly. Joy apologised profusely for 'being like that' and 'for being such hard work' and she would routinely say 'it's just the way I am'. She would be worried that people did not like her, that she would never be able to do social work and considered whether she had chosen the right career. The response from the authority was questioning whether she was 'cut out' for statutory social work and maybe she would be better off in a different PLO' (from Gibson, 2012, p. 4).

The case example is from a journal article by Matthew Gibson (2012). It is based on a student he worked with in the role of PE. The student subsequently passed this placement. Gibson used the concept (or theory) of narrative practice to analyse the dynamics of the situation on placement, when it became apparent that Joy was struggling. This helped him to form an initial assessment of what might be going wrong, but also to guide his thinking regarding how he could work together with the student to define her problem more clearly. He encouraged Joy to use her reflective log to write down the narratives (or stories) that her own family would tell about her and also the narratives that the student would tell about herself. The reflective log was used in supervision as a basis for Joy developing a greater understanding of how these narratives were impacting on her belief in herself and also linked to her anxiety at undertaking tasks on placement. Joint PE and student exploration and defining of the problem in supervision led on to the development of an agreed strategy for addressing it by supporting the student in changing the dominant negative narrative she had unconsciously given herself.

However, the PE additionally took responsibility for developing a broad plan of action that simultaneously involved several aspects of the Practice Learning System, rather than just intervening at the point of the learning partnership or supervision between student and PE. The PE utilised feedback from colleagues and service users and support from other individuals within the placement agency team to encourage the student to look at how she was filtering out positive feedback and retaining only negative messages about herself. The PE also ensured that he liaised promptly with the university so that the student could receive additional tutorial support and that a series of action plans and targets were agreed. The student was required to meet these targets in order for the placement to continue. This PE demonstrated a productive balance between supporting the student in overcoming a significant barrier to her learning while also fulfilling the assessment aspect of the PE role (link to 'Critical question 1').

When encountering difficulties on placement, the emphasis needs to be on considering the placement problem in a holistic manner, to try and identify the underlying key issues that are impacting on the student's progress on placement. TCSW in conjunction with the Higher Education Academy (HEA), have designed a 'Placement Assessment Report Template' for PEs. The template includes a section for the PE to summarise any issues or circumstances that have been taken into account by the PE in their recommendation (TCSW, 2012a, p. 2). This includes issues in relation to the personal circumstances or specific requirements of the student. The PCF (as highlighted in Chapter 6 on Assessment) supports an increased emphasis on the *process* of practice learning rather than focusing solely on outcomes. The PE therefore needs to be holistic in their approach to identifying the relative needs, strengths and weaknesses of the student throughout the course of the placement, and to actively use the whole of the Practice Learning System to support the student's placement learning. You may also wish to reflect on the degree to which you feel as a PE that any stronger aspects of a student's practice may balance out or counteract any weaker areas of their practice in terms of your overall assessment of the student's capability in relation to the nine domains (TCSW, 2012a; 2012b).

How to identify the nature of the placement difficulty

Maclean and Lloyd (2008) provide a useful checklist of prompt questions you can reflect on as a PE (outlined below) to help you identify the nature of the problem more clearly and develop a strategy or way forward for dealing with the problem(s) through action planning. Alternatively, Williams and Rutter (2010) offer a similar list of prompt questions for PEs to reflect on when placement difficulties arise. Considering one or more of the issues outlined in the checklist in relation to a particular placement you are supporting, may provide evidence towards a variety of different PEPS domains, as suggested below. In addition, these are particularly valuable for those working towards Stage 2, needing to demonstrate reflection and development.

Check issues of:

power, powerlessness and partnership in relation to the student – *have you raised and addressed these issues with the student? Have you worked in a way that is student led? (PEPS B:2; A:3);*

placement preparation (roles and responsibilities) – *has everyone involved in the place-ment received sufficient preparation for the practice learning process and are respective roles and responsibilities clear to all parties? (PEPS A:5);*

placement agreements – *are the Learning and Supervision Agreements and the plan (or curric-ulum) of learning for the student clear, or do they need revision?*

assessment – *are there any issues to do with the fairness, reliability or process of the assessment, or regarding the assessment methods used? (PEPS C:2; C:3; C:4; C:5; C:6; C:10);*

criteria – *are both yourself and the student clear about what assessment criteria will be used to assess their progress for first or final placement? (PEPS C:9);*

feedback given to the student – *has this been clear, consistent and constructive?*

specific needs – *are you aware of any specific student needs and have you addressed these within the placement context? (PEPS A:2; B:3; B:4);*

opportunities – *have the opportunities on placement been sufficient and appropriate to allow the student to demonstrate their practice competence for first or final placement? (PEPS A:3; A:7).*

(Adapted from Maclean and Lloyd, 2008, pp. 169–70)

Action planning

Where any type of placement difficulty arises, individual university procedures may differ, so it is important you familiarise yourself with the procedures specific to the university for the student you are supervising. However, in general the procedure to be followed will usually involve the following.

» The initial naming and discussing the issue of concern as soon as it arises. This will usually be raised in supervision. The shared discussion and naming of the concern should be recorded, an initial plan of action agreed, and a timescale for reviewing progress agreed. If sufficient progress is not made in addressing the concerns effectively, then it may be necessary to;

» Hold an additional placement meeting (sometimes known as a 'concerns meeting') chaired by the student's university placement tutor, to discuss any areas of concern, leading on to;

» An agreed action plan, outlining the main areas of concern and how each issue will be addressed, including timescales for implementation of each aspect of the plan. The action plan should also make clear what criteria will be used to indicate that the required outcome has been successfully achieved. The PE, on-site PS (if applicable), tutor and student should all attend this additional placement meeting and notes of the meeting should be recorded and copies given to all parties.

» A date should be set for a follow-up meeting to review the plan (usually held within 2–4 weeks of the additional placement meeting).

» At the follow up meeting, if the particular area(s) of concern are subsequently resolved and the student is 'back on track', there may be no need for any further additional meetings to be held and the rest of the placement can then continue in the usual manner.

» However, if problems remain at the follow-up meeting, there may be a need to hold a series of further action planning meetings, for some or all of the remainder of the placement, to ensure that the student's rate of progress is maintained.

» If problems remain, a 'Fail' recommendation may need to be made.

Case **example: action planning**

Karen was a social work student undertaking her first placement in an independent sector agency. Within a few weeks of the start of the placement the PS raised concerns with the off-site PE about the student's poor level of motivation, her inability to complete tasks within the suggested timescales, and an inability to work independently. The student raised concerns with the off-site PE about a lack of work or tasks available for her to complete on placement, and that she was often sitting in the office with nothing to do.

New referrals to the agency had been slow to arrive since the start of the placement and the PS had not been able to allocate as much initial assessment work to the student as she would have liked. However, she felt the student was not motivated to make the most of shadowing other team members and visiting external agencies, to help develop her knowledge base.

A three-way supervision meeting was arranged to discuss and try to address the early concerns raised regarding the slow development of some learning opportunities within the placement setting and the need for the student to demonstrate an ability to take a greater degree of responsibility for her own learning.

An action plan was drawn up that included the student being asked to organise several visits during the next two weeks to external agencies from a list provided by the PS. The importance of the student completing other tasks within required timescales in order to provide evidence of professional accountability was also emphasised. The tutor was also informed that there were some initial placement difficulties but that these were being dealt with at this stage through the holding of a three-way supervision meeting and the drawing up of an action plan.

Despite the agreed plan of action, the student appeared to continue to lack motivation and to struggle to complete some of her work according to the timescales agreed with the PS. In completing the first direct observation form, for example, the student produced it later than the agreed date, but also did not appear to be able to clearly identify which PCF domains were most relevant to her observed practice situation. Although the observation of the student's direct practice was regarded overall as 'satisfactory', there were still some key points of development identified regarding the lack of assertiveness of the student in managing the observed group work session.

With the mid-point review meeting approaching in a few weeks time, the PE and PS agreed that the student was not making satisfactory progress and that an additional placement meeting would therefore need to be held to discuss these concerns. The mid-point review meeting therefore also became a formal 'concerns meeting' held in relation to unsatisfactory student progress on placement.

Difficulties in relation to the functioning of any aspect of the Practice Learning System can occur at any point in the placement. In most instances, however, early identification of potential problems such as those relating to student learning or behaviour, barriers to learning, or to lack of suitable learning opportunities, can be remedied through the use of an action planning approach and the placement can then continue to progress towards a successful outcome. However, it is equally important to acknowledge that if concerns about a student's practice are significant or persist despite further support being offered to them, some students may need to be 'failed'.

Degrees of difficulty – what constitutes a difficulty or concern?

Professional **development prompt**

For the following numbered list of potential difficulties that might arise on placement, reflect on:

» which are the most serious potential problems;

» what specific knowledge you might need (regarding policies and procedures, PCF capabilities or theories of adult learning, for example) to help you to deal effectively with each situation;

» what potential action (if any) you or others within the Practice Learning System might have to take in relation to each issue.

1. Student not achieving the agreed target dates for the completion of placement work.

2. Serious professional misconduct by the student.

3. Lack of learning opportunities within the agency.

4. Short period of sickness or leave of PE or PS.

5. Lengthy period of sickness of PE or PS.

6. PE organisation of a planned direct observation falls through.

7. Rate of progress of student not seeming to be sufficient at the mid-placement stage.

8. Student not proactive in supervision.

9. Student extremely defensive, angry or upset when given any feed-back by the PE.

10. Student very nervous or anxious about taking the lead role in a practice situation.

The PCF level capabilities may be useful in helping you to assess the degree of concern for some of the difficulties outlined. For example, Point 8 raises the issue of a degree of student passivity in supervision. The PCF end-of-first-placement-level capabilities Domain 1 (*Professionalism*) suggest that by the end of first placement a student should be able to *recognise the important role of supervision, and make an active contribution* (TCSW, 2012h, p. 1). The PCF may therefore be something that you could use together with the student to discuss the importance of them taking an active role in the supervisory process.

In relation to Point 9, psychosocial theory may help you to critically analyse why the student might be reacting in a disproportionate manner to feedback and lead on to ideas about how to approach the student in relation to this issue. The concepts of defence mechanism, resistance and transference, are all rooted in psychoanalytic theory (Trevithick, 2005) and may be relevant. Equally, you may feel other theories are much more applicable. Other difficulties (see Point 3) may relate much more to other parts of the Practice Learning System, such as the placement agency itself and the availability or sufficiency of learning opportunities, rather being about the student's own attitudes, behaviour or performance.

Barriers to learning

Student social workers may have specific needs that need to be considered within the planning, support and assessment processes of the placement to ensure they do not have additional barriers to learning that they need to overcome within the placement setting. In situations where a student is not making satisfactory progress, however, it is especially important to revisit and explore with the student whether there are any as yet unrecognised or unacknowledged barriers that may be impacting on student progress. (Revisiting Chapter 4 on Enabling Learning may help you to reflect on the specific needs of the student in terms of their preferred learning style and identified learning needs, for example.)

The Equality Act 2010 requires all employers to make *reasonable adjustments* to the workplace for a person with a disability, and also outlines nine protected characteristics that cannot be used to treat people unfairly (Home Office, 2012). In addition, as a PE, you therefore need to remain aware of some of the structural barriers (Thompson,

1997) that may contribute to difficulties arising on placement. Research has found, for example, that there is a higher percentage fail rate on practice placements for male than for female social work students (Furness, 2012). Male students and students with disabilities have between an 8 per cent and 15 per cent lower chance (respectively) of passing their social work degree than female students or students with no disabilities (GSCC, 2009, p. 28). A higher failure rate for students from black and minority ethnic communities has also been identified as an issue in relation both to practice placements and the social work degree course in general (Bartoli *et al.*, 2008, GSCC, 2009). See Chapter 4 for a further discussion of the 'Mandela Model' (Tedam, 2012) which was devised as a tool by educators working in this context.

Trotter and Gilchrist (1996, cited in Furness and Gilligan, 2004) found that many social workers had only a limited awareness of issues of homophobia and heterosexism, and that PEs were reluctant to discuss these issues. Similarly, a reluctance of PEs to discuss issues of religion and the impact of religious or other beliefs on practice with students (Gilligan, 2003) has also been noted.

Good, satisfactory, marginal or failing?

A marginal student can be defined as a student who *is at risk of failing to reach the standard required* for the level of the placement (Brandon and Davies, 1979, p. 295).

A failing student can be defined as a student who *is a long way from demonstrating competence or in fact the student may be practising in a way which directly contravenes the required standards* (Mclean and Lloyd, 2008, p. 171).

However, it may be useful to see marginal and failing students as existing on a continuum (ranging from excellent–good–satisfactory–marginal–borderline–failing) as this acknowledges that at any point during the placement a student can potentially move in either direction along the continuum. This means being open to the possibility that a student can markedly improve or progress from a marginal or potentially failing situation, to making satisfactory progress if given the right support (see the previous case example of Joy). However, this is not to ignore that fact that a student may alternatively continue to move in the direction of an increasing level of concern regarding their progress despite a range of measures being put in place to support the student in their learning. In these instances, it is important to accept that PEs also have a duty to *effectively act as gatekeepers for entry to the profession and safeguard the interest of service users and employers alike* (Furness and Gilligan, 2004, p. 486) and may therefore need to make a 'Fail' recommendation. As a PE, you therefore need to be prepared to make a 'Fail' recommendation when you believe the student has not demonstrated capability for the relevant placement level or the student is felt to be exhibiting practice behaviours that would be regarded as dangerous or unprofessional. It is important to note that this decision would only be taken once full opportunity had been offered to the student to demonstrate capability *and* all 'concerns' procedures followed correctly.

What then constitutes sufficient or insufficient evidence of student capability? There are different requirements regarding the particular level of knowledge and skills required of students at the end of first and final practice placements. These are the relevant capabilities that you will need to consider when reflecting on the range and quality of evidence provided by the student and obtained from other sources (such as feedback from service users and agency colleagues, for example) when making both your formative and your summative assessments.

How do you then decide, as a PE, what is a 'good enough' standard for a student to achieve a 'Pass' recommendation, especially if you are feeling that a student's performance is 'marginal'? If we revisit the case of Joy, if the particular concerns outlined in the case example were viewed in isolation, you may feel that Joy was a 'marginal' student or even that she should have been 'failed'. However, taking a more holistic approach, the PE was aware there were a number of other strengths that Joy demonstrated in relation to her practice (that were also confirmed by feedback from other agency colleagues and service users). The PE therefore recognised that providing support to Joy in helping her to overcome the key barrier that was affecting her learning would ensure the student had the opportunity to successfully complete the placement. (This could be regarded as providing evidence for PEPS Domain C:14 and C:16.) For Joy the action plan was successful and she was able to make the required changes. However, if Joy had not been able to change her view of herself this may have led to the need for the PE to make a 'Fail' recommendation, as, despite her strengths, a degree of self-efficacy is still necessary for effective practice.

Self-efficacy theory is a social cognitive theory that was developed by Bandura (1986, cited in Walker *et.al*, 2008) and suggests that *whilst a person may know what actions need to be undertaken in order to successfully execute a particular task ... there needs to be an element of belief or confidence in one's ability to perform those actions in order to achieve effective completion* (p. 94).

Failing to fail students

Duffy, 2003 (cited in Shapton, 2006) identifies several reasons why PEs may fail to fail students. They include the PE feeling that they have left it too late in the placement to raise their concerns; the PE worrying about the personal consequences for the student of a 'Fail' recommendation; concerns about the negative impact on the PE themselves in terms of coping with the emotional and workload-related stress and pressure that will result from making a 'Fail' recommendation; and the degree of experience and confidence of the PE in deciding what is felt to be a 'good enough' standard of practice in order to make a 'Pass' versus a 'Fail' recommendation.

There is a range of research evidence that indicates the degree of emotional stress that can result from working with a marginal or failing placement situation, for the PE as well as for the student, should not be underestimated (Basnett and Sheffield, 2010; Finch and Taylor, 2013; Furness, 2012; Sharpe, 2000). It can potentially lead to a deterioration in the working relationship between PE and student. This issue therefore needs to be openly acknowledged, including an acceptance that both parties should be able to seek independent sources of support. Finch and Taylor (2013) cite the concept of *role strain* as being a factor in why PEs may find it difficult to fail students. The stress of undertaking and balancing the multiple roles of supporter, enabler, assessor and manager, especially when there are placement difficulties (link to 'Critical question 1') can be a considerable source of stress and conflict for PEs. Waterhouse *et al.*, (2011) similarly identified that it was often not the degree of confidence of the PE in relation to their assessment of the student that led to reluctance to make a 'Fail' recommendation, but was more often to do with *the values of social work and wanting to maximise the potential and not close out people's opportunities* (p. 107).

Some research undertaken in respect of working with marginal and failing students indicates that PEs often give their student the 'benefit of the doubt' when making their final assessment decision (Duffy, 2003). You need to reflect carefully in your role as a PE as to why you may be considering recommending a 'Pass' (but only just) when you feel a student's progress is 'marginal'.

As part of your decision making process:

>> are you making allowances in terms of lowering your assessment standard regarding what is 'good enough' practice because you are aware that some aspects of the student's learning environment or opportunities were not entirely adequate?

>> should you be making any allowances for this, or are you clear about what you would regard as a 'good enough' baseline of practice, regardless of the placement circumstances?

>> how much should you take into account specific issues that may impact on the student's learning, such as personal circumstances, for example? (link to 'Critical question 3');

>> how much are the possible negative consequences for the student in terms of your assessment decision (such as the student potentially failing the course and ending their possibility of a career in social work) affecting your judgement at final placement if a student is felt to be 'marginal'?

>> if a student has shown some degree of improvement towards the end of the placement, is this still a sufficient degree of improvement for a 'Pass' recommendation to be made, or does the student's progress still fall slightly short of a 'Pass' standard?

Factors that may indicate a marginal or failing placement

The practice learning literature contains a wealth of information about the range of factors relating to a student's skills, values, attitudes and behaviours that may be apparent in placements where a student is assessed as marginal or failing. They include a student's:

>> dependence on supervision;

>> resistance to change;

>> inability to relate the facts they are learning to the needs and demands of the situation (Finch, 2011);

>> negative attitudes and failure to engage in the practice learning experience (Moriarty *et al.*, 2010);

>> poor communication and interpersonal skills;

>> poor understanding of the social work role;

>> lack of motivation and unwillingness to learn (Burgess *et al.*, 1998);

>> persistent lateness;

>> lack of personal insight or lack of insight into professional boundaries (Duffy, 2003);

>> a lack of ability to form relationships or to show empathy (Lishman, 2012b).

Furness and Gilligan (2004) additionally outline a list of behaviours that would generally be regarded as incompatible with a student passing their practice placement and becoming a qualified social worker.

They include:

>> damage to service users;

» crossing professional boundaries;

» disrespect of service users;

» controlling service users;

» putting service users in danger, and;

» not using supervision.

However, Furness and Gilligan (2004) also found that there was no common agreement between the social work professionals they consulted in their research as to which of these behaviours were incompatible with passing a student at final level, as the list of behaviours were open to different levels of interpretation. As a PE you therefore have to accept that any judgement that you make about 'good enough' or 'unsatisfactory' practice will necessarily be qualitative in nature. In order to ensure your judgement is both fair and valid, it is therefore important to be open to other perspectives and viewpoints and consult with others in order to test out validity and fairness of your assessment. Chapter 6 on 'Assessment' outlines the key principles of good practice in respect of both formative and summative assessment. Collating assessment evidence over the course of the whole placement, using a range of different sources and assessment methods, is good practice for all practice placements. However, adopting these assessment practices will also ensure that you will always have a strong evidence base from which you can justify and evidence your assessment decisions when also working with marginal and failing placement situations.

Most of the factors identified so far regarding marginal and failing placements focus on concerns relating to the student's own behaviour, skills, values, and knowledge base. However, some of the practice learning research undertaken also indicates that the PE's own poor supervisory skills, unclear communication and poor assessment ability, may also be significant factors in failed placements (Burgess *et al.*, 1998). The PE's ability to facilitate learning, manage the placement, promote reflection, and to teach and link theory to practice, are key aspects that affect the quality of placement learning from the perspective of social work students (Lefevre, 2005). Placement problems were often identified as resulting from an *expectations clash* (Lefevre, 2005 p. 576) between some or all of the parties within the learning partnership, rather than being the result of what some might term a 'personality clash' between student and PE. In fact the term 'personality clash' should be recognised as an unhelpful concept that is best avoided as it diverts discussion away from a more objective analysis and direct naming of the issues of concern. Poor communication and management of the learning experience, poor placement support, and relationship and supervisory issues in respect of all parties involved in learning system, were also often a feature of placements that broke down (Dove and Skinner, 2010).

There can be additional complexity involved in managing placements where an off-site PE model is used. While the involvement of four different individuals (student, tutor, on-site PS and PE) within the learning partnership can enable the student to benefit from a richer range of skills, knowledge and experience, the PE needs to ensure that the needs and expectations of all parties are met regarding mutual clarity of respective roles, tasks and responsibilities in order to ensure the placement functions effectively (Lawson, 1998). The need for regular three-way meetings is therefore essential to ensure any issue or concerns are discussed promptly and openly. This may include, for example, the need to negotiate the existence of different opinions on the student's rate of progress between on-site PS and off-site PE.

Weighing up the evidence

Thompson (2006b) offers a simple but effective tool for helping the PE to 'weigh the evidence' when making their assessment decision regarding sufficient or insufficient student progress. He outlines a list of both positive and negative indicators for assessing each aspect of a student's practice in nine separate areas: professional values and attitudes; communication skills; assessment skills; intervention skills; use of supervision; ability to relate theory to practice; self-management skills; ability to work within the agency framework; and development as a social worker; for both first and final placement levels. For example, in repect of a student's professional values and attitudes during their first placement, Thompson cites the following as positive indicators of student practice:

Shows awareness of importance of values, beliefs and attitudes on part of both worker and client; recognises significance of power and authority in familial, group and worker/client relationships; flexible and open-minded in matters of value, opinion and judgement; shows a commitment to providing an equally valid service to all clients; is moving towards a considered personal and professional value base; involves clients/service users in the process.

(Thompson, 2006b, p.128)

Thompson similarly provides a list of negative indicators of student progress during their first placement in relation to values and attitudes:

Denies, disregards or fails to recognise contribution of values, beliefs, attitudes; tends to ignore, overlook or be unquestioning of issues of power and authority; is rigid, dogmatic or over-assertive in matters of value, opinion and judgement; allows prejudice or judgemental attitudes to affect work; confuses fact and opinion; advocates, condones or engages in elements of discrimination within practice and policy; does not involve clients/service users in the process.

(Thompson, 2006b, p.128)

You may find Thompson's positive and negative indicators for first and final placement a useful checklist to use to examine your own expectations and assumptions regarding the standards you think a student at first and final placement should be achieving. However, you could equally devise your own list of what you feel are positive and negative indicators of 'good enough' practice by using the PCF level capabilities for first and final level placements to guide you and then comparing and discussing your expectations with other PE colleagues.

In weighing the evidence you may also need to consider what is regarded as 'good enough' practice in terms of the work requirements of a particular placement agency and whether this is the same as what is 'good enough' in order for the student to demonstrate professional capability at the required level (Finch and Taylor, 2013), especially with regard to qualifying social worker level capabilities.

Conclusion

The National Organisation for Practice Teaching (NOPT, 2013) has published a *Code of Practice for PEs* that contains good practice guidance regarding the management of marginal or failing placements.

This includes:

The PE ensuring that they highlight, at the beginning of the placement, what processes will be undertaken if the student appears to be failing to meet the required standards.

Making a commitment to share with the student any concern about their level of practice competence and to work openly to reach agreement with the student on how competence may be achieved.

The PE to be open to examining his or her own practice to explore whether the concern may be based on any form of discrimination, or if student progress is being impeded by any oppressive aspect of the placement.

If a student is failing, the PE should encourage the student to seek an independent source of support.

The PE to utilise the practice learning support structures appropriately, to seek guidance as necessary, and to work within the relevant social work programme procedures.

(Adapted from NOPT, 2013, p. 11)

What does the research say?

There is a whole range of research available in journal articles focusing on different aspects of working with placement difficulties. For example, there is research that explores the emotional impact of failing a student on the PE (Finch and Taylor, 2013); the needs of PEs (Sharpe, 2000, Waterhouse *et al.*, 2011) and the coping and problem-solving strategies that PEs develop to cope with the emotional stresses of dealing with a failing placement (Basnett and Sheffield, 2010).

However, the two pieces of research I have chosen to focus on are one that explores what is 'good enough' practice in the assessment of social work students (Furness and Gilligan, 2004), and another that highlights the impact of personal, cultural and structural factors in respect of student experiences of practice learning (Bartoli *et al.*, 2008).

Furness and Gilligan research

Furness and Gilligan (2004) published their research in the form of a journal article that explores both what constitutes 'good enough' practice in the assessment of social work students and what factors influence PE assessment of students.

> » *Sample* – Over 70 PEs, tutors and placement co-ordinators.

> » *Data collection* – via a consultation undertaken during a regional conference.

Key messages highlighted in the research

That there were many different views as to what constituted 'good enough' practice for both first and final placements. There was also no clear consensus as to what behaviour or characteristics should result in *permanent exclusion for entering or re-entering the profession* (Furness and Gilligan, 2004, p. 469). As PE judgements were recognised as being qualitative in nature, it was felt to be important for PEs to ensure that they consulted with others to help them form and reflect on their judgements, to avoid prejudice or too great a degree of subjectivity.

In relation to assessing 'good enough ' practice, it was identified as important that PEs should be able to clearly identify the reasons for their assessment, to supply clear evidence for these from a range of sources, and to relate their opinions to specific practice or value requirements. The issue of students sometimes being given the 'benefit of the doubt', particularly at the end of first placement by unsupported or inexperienced PEs, was raised. This often led to a student being assessed as a borderline 'Pass' rather than a 'Fail'. The research also raises the issue of adequate funding for practice placements such that additional resources are available for practice placements in circumstances where there are students facing specific personal difficulties, or in relation to students with disabilities or other specific needs. This research highlights the more general need for PEs to be able to consider the specific needs of each individual student within their assessment and to identify and respond to any *special issues* (TCSW/HEA, 2012, p. 11) that may impact on student progress on placement such as health, personal circumstances or disability, for example.

Bartoli, Kennedy and Tedam research

Bartoli, Kennedy and Tedam (2008) published their research in the form of a journal article, summarising their findings from an exploration of Black African students' experiences of practice learning. This was in response to the high failure rate identified in relation to practice placements for Black African students.

> » *Sample* – 15 Black African social work students from a UK university, whose country of origin was Africa, the place where their 'formative education' was also undertaken (Bartoli *et al.*, 2008, p. 78). Three of these students were considered to be 'international' students and 12 were considered to be 'home' students due to their period of residency within the UK and their qualification for receipt of a GSCC bursary.

> » *Data collection* – via a focus group, or via an individual interview for those that could not attend the focus group.

Key messages highlighted in the research

Some of the emerging themes included; gender roles and expectations; a lack of practice experience relating to unfamiliarity with UK systems; students' motivation to study social work; personal circumstances; homesickness and culture shock; differing expectations related to different cultural norms; and experiences of individual and institutional racism.

Gender role expectations, finances and health

All of the Black African students had family responsibilities for others who were financially dependent on them either in the UK, or in terms of sending money back to family members in Africa. Many of the students had to undertake part-time employment in addition to their studies and family responsibilities. Some students were also being sponsored by family members or friends, adding an additional pressure regarding their fear of failure. International students do not qualify for the travel bursary that is available to other social work students, adding additional financial pressure. Personal circumstances such the bereavement of a close family member in Africa (for several students), involved significant travel expenses and payment of funeral expenses and a degree of restriction on the ability to grieve, due to the pressure to complete the course. Emotional and physical health problems were also present for all the students involved in the research.

Homesickness, lack of practice experience and cultural diversity

Several students found the separation from family members difficult, adding to their feelings of social isolation. There was also a degree of 'culture shock' experienced by students who had arrived in the UK more recently, in relation to the comparative levels of social need and access to services offered in the UK as compared with the student's own experiences. Contextualising the UK welfare state framework, bureaucratic organisational structures, thresholds and theoretical social work models and methods, was difficult when these were so different from the student's own personal experiences. Often additional help, strategies or support to facilitate students in adjusting were not offered. A conflict of culturally based values could also arise on placement between the 'Western' cultural values and other Black African cultural norms – such as deference to those in authority, for example.

Motivation to study and experience of individual and institutional racism

Some students felt they were being discriminated against by their practice teachers/ assessors. This took the form of being monitored more closely than other white students, hindering their ability to progress. Other students cited instances of unequal treatment such as stereotyping, or being mistrusted and patronised.

The findings from this research study identified the need for social work courses to consider implementing a range of strategies to support Black African students that included peer support groups, mentoring, incorporation of more international perspectives in teaching content, and for practice examples used to demonstrate social work theories and methods to consider incorporating an African-centric as well as a Euro-centric paradigm.

Taking it further

Chapter 9 of **Beverley and Worsley** (2007) deals with difficulties on placement. The chapter provides an analysis of a range of factors that can lead to placement difficulties arising, and explores how to deal with these. They include; differences in expectations and perceptions; differing opinions about competence; unhelpful supervision processes; and student resistance to learning.

Chapters 7 and 8 of **Thompson** (2006b) offer a useful resource to PEs. Chapter 7 provides a valuable tool that PEs can either use directly as a guide for their assessment of a student, or can adapt for their own use. Thompson offers a list of positive and negative indicators in respect of the holistic assessment of social work students in relation to their knowledge base, values and practice skills – for first and final level placements. Chapter 8 uses a range of different case examples to illustrate placement problems that can commonly arise and how to deal with them, as well as what pitfalls to avoid.

Marsh *et al.* (no date), *Assessment of Students in Health and Social Care: Managing Failing Students in Practice*, is an online resource that is particularly useful for exploring the role of action planning and feedback when problems arise, and also provides an action plan template.

The material in this chapter links to the following PEPS domains and values statements for PEs and supervisors:

Learning outcome domains required for Stage 1 and Stage 2 PEs

A:7; A:8; B:1; B:2; B:3; B:4; B:8; all of Domain C

Additional learning outcome domains required for Stage 2 PEs

B:10; all of Domain D

Values for PEs and supervisors: 1–7

Chapter aims

- » To enable PEs to explore what reflective practice means to them.

- » To help PEs use reflective practice and critical thinking to consolidate their assessment of the student's capability.

- » To offer PEs methods to use with students to facilitate development of skills in critical reflection with a focus on outcomes for service users.

Critical **questions**

- » How do I embed a reflective and critical approach into my work with a student?

- » How do I model reflective practice for my student in the context of a challenging working environment?

- » How do I help a student reflect in the best way for them?

Introduction

Throughout the previous chapters it has become evident that much of the facilitation of learning and assessment of capability of a student is dependent upon reflective practice. It is the view of the authors that reflection and critical analysis form the glue that holds the teaching and assessment process together. We have therefore positioned this chapter later in the book in order to be able to answer some of the questions raised, to help the PE consolidate their practice with a student, and to prompt serious thought about their own CPD, especially in moving to Stage 2 of the PEPS. The chapter will briefly review key concepts within the broad domain of reflective practice but does not set out to add to the wealth of literature in this field. Instead the section 'Taking it further' at the end of the chapter will signpost the reader to some material that we have found useful.

Having reviewed key threads and definitions, the chapter will examine the place of reflective practice within social work and remind the reader of how the new professional frameworks require the application of reflective and critical thinking. It will offer a guide for PEs in helping students develop the requisite skills and in assessing confidently that their students have the capability to critically apply their learning to contexts other than their current learning environment. This latter seems to the authors to be the nub of what 'holistic and progressive' assessment requires of PEs. In other words we want to ask the question *how do I know what my student is thinking and how do I ensure that they are thinking in a way which will ensure safe and effective practice for service users?* Furthermore, if a PE produces a well evidenced final report on a student based on holistic assessment principles (see Chapter 6), that in turn should contribute evidence of the PE's own reflective practice in order to support an application for Stage 2 status.

It is useful at this point to consider some terms and concepts central to discussions about reflection and its use in developing practice.

Reflective practice

While there is no commonly accepted definition of reflective practice, there is a well established agreement about the essential components; these include reviewing and analysing an experience, drawing conclusions and incorporating them into future actions. In social work the desired outcome is usually the development of best practice for service users' benefit and professional development for practitioners. Boud et al. (1985, p. 19) talked about reflection as an activity where you, *recapture (your) experience, think about it, mull it over and evaluate it.* Clouder (2000, cited in Maclean 2010, p. 10) develops this to define reflective practice thus: *[reflective practice] ... involves the critical analysis of everyday working practices to improve competence and promote professional development.*

Critical reflection

Social work is a complex and uncertain activity, facing the practitioner with continually changing demands and expectations. Critical reflection implies therefore *open-minded, reflective approaches that take account of different perspectives, experiences and assumptions* (Glaister in Fraser and Matthews, 2012, p. 8). It entails the ability to practise with a sound evidence base, while being able to develop new approaches and knowledge in response to changing contexts. Authors such as Fook (2002) point out that critical reflection can uncover structural issues and imbalances of power which will in turn demand of the student a broader understanding of social, political and legal contexts.

Reflexivity

The discussion can be taken further with a consideration of reflexivity. This is defined by Taylor and White (2000) as an activity which involves reflection not just on the individual's actions but also on the professional and social context in which they are operating: *For workers in health and welfare it means that they subject knowledge claims and practice to analysis* (p. 206).

The purpose of the above section is to encourage the PE to clarify the terms used within social work practice and education and through further reading to become more aware of the skills and knowledge needed to exercise reflection at different levels. Throughout the rest of the chapter the term reflective practice will be applied in a general sense to mean the activity of reviewing, analysing and learning from experience, with all the critical awareness that this implies. The PCF has been designed to reflect the interrelatedness of theory, knowledge, skills and values, and it is therefore axiomatic that the student will need to develop skills of analysis in order to make sense of their practice. In their own, parallel venture, the PE will need to deconstruct their own practice in order to teach the student and more importantly to be able to assess holistically. Biggs (2007), in commenting on holistic assessment, explains *we arrive at [such judgements] by understanding the whole in the light of the parts*, and that *the assessment is of the integrated action, not of the performance of each part* (p. 5)

Doel (TCSW, 2012a, p. 5) elaborates further, arguing that we need both partial and contextual understanding of practice. By partial he means *a detailed understanding of the various behavioural competences which constitute practice*. Contextual for him involves *an awareness of how practice is influenced by time and place; and at a social level this is an understanding of structural influences on practice.*

We can thus begin to see how reflective practice is key for the PE in their role.

Why is reflective practice important?

Without doubt, reflective practice is one of the key concepts that practice educators will employ, both in terms of the tools they use to develop learners, but also how they develop themselves as educators. Reflective practice is important in the development of professional practice as it enables us to learn from our experiences of working with others. Developing reflective practice means developing ways of reviewing our own practice so that whilst it becomes a routine it is further a process by which we might continuously develop ... from a compliance to a learning culture.

(Munro, 2011, p. 5)

This links to 'Critical question 2' posed at the beginning of the chapter – *How do I model reflective practice for my student in the context of a challenging working environment?* What Munro is advocating here is that the PE should devote and make time for reflection – this will not only develop their own practice as PE and practitioner but models good practice for the student.

As indicated elsewhere in the book, the social work reforms (DfE 2009; DfE 2010) were informed partly by a perception of the inadequacies of social work practice and an attempt by the profession to counteract the growth of a managerialist approach to social work focused more on outcomes than process. *Students themselves need, through taking the degree, to begin developing into social workers who reflect critically on what they do and the decisions they* make (DfE 2009, p. 19)

The resultant frameworks regulating and guiding social workers' practice make explicit that the development and application of skills of reflection and critical analysis are cornerstones of effective and safe practice. The SOPS (HCPC 2012a) highlight the prominence given to these skills. They are framed throughout in terms such as *be aware of, reflect on, draw on,* thus assuming a level of analysis and reflection in social workers. Standards 11–14 refer specifically to skills of analysis, reflection and application of knowledge. The PCF, in introducing a specific domain relating to 'Critical Reflection and Analysis', cannot be more clear in its intention to bring to the fore learning and development in this aspect of a social worker's professional identity. Finally the PEPS (TCSW, 2013b) require PEs *to contribute to the learning and development of the agency as a training organization* (Domain A:8), *teach the learner ... demonstrating the ability for critical reflection* (Domain B:1), and *demonstrate critical reflection on their own development as practice educators including the use of feedback* (Domain D:2).

'Because' is not enough: working towards a shared understanding of why reflective practice is important

It is acknowledged that doing something because we are told we have to is not enough of a justification when working with learners. The requirements and guidance above are a reflection of the plethora of research, practice wisdom and theory that underpin the now largely uncontested conclusion that applying an approach broadly called 'reflective practice' is vital for effective social work. In terms, too, of the student's professional development, *deep* learning (Marton and Saljo (1976) in Williams and Rutter, 2010), cannot be promoted or achieved without critical thinking to enable information to be assimilated and applied in new circumstances. For facilitators of social work practice learning, an essential first step early in placement is to ascertain what the student's understanding of reflective practice is and why it is an essential part of their own practice and your assessment of them. This will require you to know your own approach to reflective practice.

Professional **development prompt: setting the scene**

Ask yourself the following questions.

» Why is reflective practice important for social workers?

» When do I reflect?

» How do I reflect?

» Have I an example of when reflective practice has helped me make sense of a situation?

» How do I take into account the service users I work with in my reflection?

Exercise:

You may then undertake the same conversation with a student.

Your conclusions around the first question are likely to include established concepts such as accountability, professional development, improved outcomes for service users, ensuring ethical practice, among others (Maclean, 2010). These may be underpinned by reference to specific texts or articles about reflective practice (see 'Taking it further' at the end of this chapter), but given that the placement is the interface between academic and practice learning, (Knott and Scragg, 2010), the PE can perhaps contribute more to the student's development at this early stage by giving examples from practice, thus modelling reflection 'in' and 'on' action (Schon 1983) for the student. The questions about 'how' and 'when' reflection takes place may raise issues about context, organisations, personal learning styles and skills that we will seek to address later in this chapter.

As mentioned above reflective practice is not to be viewed as an isolated, individual or sporadic activity but as a core component of a joint approach to working with service users. Modelling of reflective practice should extend to the whole learning environment. Chapters 3, 4 and 5 explore how an individual PE can engage in promoting a positive learning environment; this can involve reflective activities such as group supervision. It is acknowledged that fragmented working environments, challenges around service reconfiguration, uncertainty about role, and so forth, can undermine a critically reflective approach to practice resulting in reactive rather than proactive activity undertaken with a mind to procedure rather than process: the *routinised, mechanistic practices shorn of any creativity, vision or insight* referred to by Thompson (Thompson and Pascal, 2011, p. 20). For this reason alone the PE cannot allow this approach to be mirrored within their role. More importantly, the PE cannot confidently assess a student's practice without an inherently reflective approach to their role. Thus the placement process needs to be designed in a way that promotes the involvement of the student in what we might term a 'reflective feedback loop' from the beginning. Previous chapters have referred to the relationship of the PE and student as being a core element; supervision being the arena where the most productive exchanges for learning and assessment may take place. Likewise, principles of good practice in assessment imply a self-aware, continually learning student, which is not possible without the constant review of learning opportunities and progress.

Making reflection central to the evidence of capability

TCSW has produced guidance on evidencing and recording holistic assessment. Evidence of *the ability to reflect critically* is recommended (TCSW, 2012m, p. 2). This has led social work degree programmes to revise the student placement portfolio, including in many cases introducing a specific task that requires the student to demonstrate critical analysis. You may find that the placement documentation now includes the following, more reflective, elements.

> » Practice Learning Agreement placing emphasis on the student identifying development needs and priorities.

» Mid-point review including emphasis on development and planning for the second half of the placement.

» Direct observation reports reflecting a collaborative approach to analysing learning and incorporating service user perspective.

» Service user and colleague feedback being required – emphasising the importance of the learning environment.

» Critical Analysis of Practice or Critical Incident tasks being included. ***

» Final reports being approached holistically with contributions from the student.

» Supervision Agreements and templates for recording supervision which encourage making time for reflection and discussion.

*** One north-west group of universities has developed a Critical Analysis of Practice (CAP) template to be used with each major piece of work undertaken, to promote dialogue and recording of progress around a range of issues such as planning, reflection 'for' action (Schon 1983), values and ethics, service user perspective, application of theory. These documents are intended to be used flexibly, as agreed, to provide PEs and students with the means to evaluate developing reflective capability and professional awareness as well as a tool for formative and/or summative assessment.

It should be concluded that capability cannot be assessed or evidenced without a critically reflective approach to the whole process.

How to promote reflective practice in students

Know your student

Maclean (2010) points out that learning and reflection are closely, if not inextricably, linked. She refers to the Kolb learning cycle as the archetypal adult learning theory which assumes that no learning can take place without reflection. Chapter 4 of this book also explores this notion. Given that most individuals can learn, it may be helpful as an educator to assume that most individuals therefore can reflect. It would be the authors' hypothesis that everyone reflects in one way or another and thus that it is the PE's role to enable the student to reflect in the most productive way for them. Just as PEs in training seem readily to recognise and identify with the idea of learning styles and how learning opportunities can be tailored to utilise or challenge different preferred approaches, so we would suggest the notion of preferred methods of reflection should be embraced and acted upon within the supervisory relationship. This, of course, applies equally to the PE as to the student.

Maclean (2010, p. 36) continues her examination of the Kolb learning cycle and its parallels with the Honey and Mumford (1992) delineation of learning styles to give examples of how a PE can use coaching skills to assist a student to move fully around the cycle – assuming that certain stages of the process are easier than others and thus aiming to prevent stagnation around one stage.

Tools for encouraging reflection

It follows that if we are sensitive to the preferred learning style of our student and to their approach to learning and the supervisory relationship we should take care to ensure that we encourage them to reflect and demonstrate their thinking in a way that maximises their existing skills and develops their areas of weakness.

Making use of reflective logs

Students on social work courses are generally required to produce written reflections and to maintain a personal development log or file. It is also a common expectation that they should produce regular reflective logs while on placement. There is little doubt that in order to make sense of, and learn from, an experience it is necessary to record it. However, we would encourage PEs to view the reflective log as a real and invaluable tool in moving a student from experience to learning by means of making explicit their thought processes and feelings. As Thompson and Pascal remind us, there is little learning (or assessment of capability) to be gained in viewing a reflective log as a daily list of activities undertaken.

Reflective practice is not simply a matter of pausing for thought from time to time. Rather, it is a much more sophisticated process of integrating personal and professional knowledge with the demands of the situation as part of an intelligent and creative approach to practice.

(Thompson and Pascal, 2011, p. 20)

It follows therefore that to promote the essence of reflection to aid learning, in producing their reflective log the student may benefit from using a model of reflection or becoming habituated to responding to particular questions or prompts which should, over time, become internalised. We would not wish here to prescribe a structure. You may have considered some of these on your initial training or you may find that your local social work programme or practice learning co-ordinator will offer or suggest particular models or templates to use; most will be based loosely on the accepted cycles of learning or reflection such as Gibbs (1988) or Kolb (1984). The use of the log should be mutually agreed between student and PE as part of the Practice Learning Agreement. You may wish to consider the following principles as a guide when agreeing its use.

» Regular completion.

» Focus on significant experiences – both positive and less positive.

» Agree a structure or format which encourages a critical approach and allows learning to be made explicit.

» Use the log for exploration of personal and professional development.

» Promote the log as a means of questioning and critiquing the learning environment.

» Agree the frequency and sampling of the log; by whom, when and in what format?

» Be clear on how the log is to be used for assessment of the student's learning.

In summary, the reflective log, while perhaps not forming part of the student's formal portfolio, can be a vital strand of communication between student and PE; this pertains particularly if the PE is off-site. Furthermore, as a log is reviewed throughout placement the student's development can be seen and recurring themes can be noted, which can then be brought back into the 'reflective feedback loop'.

Other tools and strategies

The next section provides a summary of suggested models and techniques for promoting reflection in a student. It should, however, be emphasised that as a social work practitioner you will be well experienced in enabling a reflective conversation through your communication, listening and assessment skills, employing techniques such as paraphrasing, clarification, probing, summarising and silence (see Chapter 5 for more exploration of supervision and the establishment of an enabling relationship).

Reflective questions

Brockbank and McGill (2007) framed questions based on the five 'Ws' (Who, Why, What, Where, When – and How) to act as instigators of a reflective approach. This may be an easy way for uncertain students to approach reflection. Questions would be designed in line with the stage of intervention or learning relevant at the time. For example, reflective questions at the planning stage of work might be directed at:

» focussing on the key issues;

» assisting students to take responsibility for their plans;

» Identifying specific actions to be taken.

'What' questions therefore might include:

» what do you want to achieve?

» what is the framework for the interview you are planning?

» what might happen if you ...?

» what might get in the way?

Models of 'structured reflection'

Maclean (2010) asserts that Schon's influential work on *reflecting 'in', 'on' and 'for' action* (Schon, 1983) has provided the template for subsequent models of reflection, which include those by Gibbs (1988), Johns (2000), Borton (1970), among others. Students and PEs may find it helpful to refer to these as templates; others may be more confident in taking the essential elements and developing conversations or written reflections more independently (see the section on 'Taking it further' for more details).

Frameworks which encourage transference of learning

If a student appears to be 'stuck' or unable to apply their learning or existing knowledge to other contexts (an essential feature of our holistic assessment), the following suggested activities may be helpful. These exercises may also assist in helping a student develop capability within those PCF domains that particularly require a broader awareness of context and socio-political factors.

» *'What if?' scenarios* – this involves hypothetically changing one aspect of the situation in order to help the student think more broadly about their practice.

» *PCS analysis* – this refers to the theoretical framework associated with Thompson (2006) that describes oppression and discrimination operating at three levels: personal, (individual values, beliefs, choices), cultural (institutional practices, stereotypes, taken-for-granted assumptions), structural (social divisions, such as race, class, gender).

» *Critical Incident Analysis* – associated most closely with Fook (2002), who develops the model to retain a focus on issues of power, inequality, oppression and exclusion.

Other methods of reflection

The methods suggested so far rely heavily on a student being articulate in speaking as well as writing. It will be helpful for you as PE to think about other ways of engaging the student in accessing their thoughts and feelings and making sense of them. Suggestions may include:

» mind mapping (helpful for a student who learns visually or has difficulties in organising thoughts);

» role-playing (useful for a student who has difficulty tuning in to the thoughts or feelings of others);

» using exercises such as recalling significant stepping stones in life – perhaps in diagrammatic form.

Involving service users in reflection

As already discussed one of the main functions of reflective practice is to ensure the effectiveness of the service we provide to service users. There is likely to be a requirement for the PE to demonstrate that service users' feedback has been taken into account within the teaching, learning and assessment of the student on placement. It is useful to pause at this point and consider how specifically the service user's voice can be heard and become integrated into reflection.

In addition to the usual opportunities for feedback (after direct observations; after interventions have taken place), one possible route to more meaningful reflection could be to arrange a special supervision where PE, service user and student collaborate in a planned discussion focused on adding the service user perspective to an experience. This would provide an opportunity for the student and PE to hear the service user's experience first hand, and also – and perhaps just as important – to allow the student to test out their own assumptions against reality.

Secondary sources can also be a rich source of service user perspectives and experience. You could ask the student to research material about service user views on service delivery in your particular area of practice. The student can then use that to test the specific experiences of the service users they are working directly with.

Conclusion

The aim of this chapter was to explore how reflective practice frames and holds together the process of enabling learning and assessment of a student. It is a belief strongly held by the authors that the true skill of an effective PE lies in unlocking the responses of a student to their experiences and in so doing promoting a reflective approach to learning and improving practice for service users. The discussion of the features of a critical thinker in Rolfe *et al.* (2011: 69) provides an excellent summary of behaviours and attitudes embodied in the reflective practitioner, that we would as PEs hope to offer to our students as a model (see 'Taking it further' at the end of the chapter).

It is hoped that being persuaded of the value of this will motivate PEs to pay attention to their own reflections and to create space and energy for this most important of activities alongside their students.

What does the research say?

Recognising that stress and burnout is a feature of social work, a research study by Gail Kinman and Louise Grant (2011) explored particular 'protective' factors that promoted resilience in trainee social workers and helped to protect them from the negative impact of the demands they faced.

» *Sample* – 240 trainee social work students (69 per cent first year students and 31 per cent second year students) completed a range of questionnaires.

» *Data collection* – via completion of online questionnaires that were designed to measure levels of emotional intelligence; the student's reflective ability; the student's empathy and social competence and their resilience to psychological distress.

Key messages highlighted in the research

1. students whose emotional and social competences were more highly developed were more resilient to stress.

2.   Those students who had increased emotional intelligence and were more adept at perceiving and appraising emotion in others, as well as in expressing (and regulating) their own emotions, were more resilient to stress.

3.   Reflective abilities were an important predictor of resilience to stress – those students who were better able to reflect on their thoughts, feelings and beliefs were more resilient to stress.

The findings from this study suggest that emotional intelligence and enhanced reflective abilities are not only helpful for improved professional practice but also act as a self-protective mechanism. The authors recognise that, within social work, there are a wide range of 'stressors' such as high workloads, paperwork, etc., but maintain that a consideration of the factors that promote resilience can enhance the well-being of students and employees. They point to the *importance of personal reflection, empathetic reflection and reflective communication* as key to enhancing resilience to stress (Kinman and Grant, 2011, p. 271)

Kinman, G. and Grant, L. (2011) 'Exploring Stress Resilience in Trainee Social Workers: The Role of Emotional and Social Competences', *British Journal of Social Work*, 41(2), pp. 261–75.

Taking it further

Knott, C. and Scragg, T. (2010) *Reflective Practice in Social Work*, 2nd edition, Exeter: Learning Matters. This book is useful for students embarking on practice learning and for PEs as a refresher. Chapter 1 is particularly useful as a review of the development and relevance of reflective practice in social work as well as a discussion of core activities to promote reflection.

Maclean, S. (2010) *The Social Work Pocket Guide to Reflective Practice*, Lichfield: Kirwin Maclean Associates Ltd. An extremely accessible guide to the history of reflective practice, characteristics of the reflective practitioner and a detailed examination of useful exercises, models and activities to assist in enabling reflection.

Thompson, N. and Pascal J. (2011) Taylor and Francis online: Reflective practice: an existentialist perspective: *Reflective Practice: International and Multidisciplinary Perspectives*, vol 12, issue 1. A very interesting yet easy-to-read exploration of the parallels between existentialism and reflective practice. It contains useful comparisons and explanations of aspects of reflection and their relation to a wider social context.

Rolfe, G., Jasper, M. and Freshwater, D. (2011) *Critical reflection in Practice*, 2nd edition, London: Palgrave Macmillan. Chapter 4 is concerned with understanding critical writing – a skill which students are asked to demonstrate through their reflective logs and other written tasks in their portfolios. This chapter helps the PE to assist a student in developing this skill and provides a helpful summary of attributes of the critical thinker.

The material in this chapter links to the following PEPS domains and values statements for PEs and supervisors:

Learning outcome domains required for Stage 1 and Stage 2 Practice Educators Domains A–D

Values for PEs and supervisors: 1–7

Chapter aims

> » To consider the requirements of the PCF; the HCPC and the PEPS (TCSW, 2013b) in relation to the CPD of practitioners and PEs.

> » To consider how the requirements of Stage 1 and Stage 2 assessment (PEPS, TCSW, 2013b) may be met.

> » To consider how the PE may maintain, develop and apply their learning as both practitioner and PE.

Critical **questions**

> » CPD – what do I want to achieve? What are the further professional development opportunities for me?

> » How do I create a learning culture and model a positive approach to CPD to my student within current challenging circumstances?

> » How can I integrate my learning into my practice – what strategies can I use and what support can I call upon?

Introduction

As was noted in Chapter 1, this book has been written in a period of change for social work and Practice Education. Throughout the book the achievement and development of professional standards in relation to the PE have been considered against the backdrop of this changing landscape, including the professional development framework of the PCF and the specific and specialist requirements of the PEPS (TCSW, 2013b). This chapter will continue this theme and will locate the PE's CPD within the wider framework of the PCF; the requirements of HCPC social work registration; and the new approach to CPD outlined by TCSW (2012j).

The chapter will also consider the requirements of the PEPS (TCSW, 2013b) and how the PE may prepare for their own assessment at Stage 1 and Stage 2, including preparation for and incorporating feedback from the direct observation of the PE's practice. In relation to Stage 2 of the PEPS (TCSW, 2013b), Domain D and the ways in which the PE's effective continuing performance and development can be demonstrated will be discussed, along with consideration of how the PE can maintain their currency of practice and enhance and develop their practice within new and related roles.

The changing landscape and the expectations on practitioners and PEs

The PCF

The PCF, as the developmental framework within which all social workers operate and progress throughout their careers, has been called the 'scaffold' that should inform the CPD requirements of social workers (TCSW, 2012j) and contains requirements within Domain 9 (Professional Leadership) relating to the learning and development of others. At Social Worker level, practitioners are expected to contribute to the learning of others. As a PE you have chosen to do this via the specialist and specific role of Practice Educator and the assessment and management of the placements of prequalifying social work students and, as such, you are required to meet the Practice Educator Standards (PEPS, TCSW, 2013b). Other social workers who do not follow the specialist pathway of PE can meet the requirements of Domain 9 in a number of ways – for example, offering support and shadowing opportunities to social work students on placement; observing their practice and giving feedback or offering joint working opportunities to social work students within their team or other teams. At Experienced Social Work level these requirements are expanded; practitioners are expected to both assess and manage the work of social work students at prequalifying level and to meet Practice Educator Standards Stage 2 (PEPS, TCSW, 2013b) and also to contribute to the learning or assess those post qualified, such as NQSWs.

HCPC registration

The PCF and the PEPS (TCSW, 2013b) expect social workers to maintain and develop their professional development and learning relevant to their area of practice – to *always be a learner* – and this is also a requirement of their continuing HCPC registration. The HCPC requires that practitioners maintain a record of their CPD activities and that they can demonstrate (if requested) how their CPD activities have impacted upon their knowledge and contributed to the development of their practice and the benefit of the service user (TCSW, 2012j). The role of PE allows ample opportunities for the demonstration of the development of the practitioner's knowledge and practice, and it is recommended (PEPS, TCSW, 2013b) that PEs record their role as a PE, and any learning, training and developmental activities they undertake relevant to the PE role within their CPD record. Suggestions as to what such CPD activities might include are discussed below.

The 'new' approach to CPD

CPD has long been considered essential for social workers and since the demise of the GSCC's Post Qualifying framework, a new approach to CPD has been outlined by TCSW (2012j). This approach recognises that both practitioners and their employers have responsibility for ensuring that there are opportunities for CPD activities and also that practitioners should be supported in their CPD endeavours. A wide range of learning and professional development activities are promoted within this new approach and it recognises that alongside 'formal' routes of training and learning – courses and academic post qualifying awards accredited by universities – there are other learning activities that practitioners can undertake that contribute to their ongoing CPD.

In your role as a PE it is likely that you have undertaken, or could undertake, a range of learning activities. Some of these will be those that you undertake on your own, others will be those where you participate as a team or group of practitioners and they will probably be a mixture of formal and informal activities. The range of learning activities and professional development opportunities that contribute to your CPD are:

> » Undertaking the PE course of training itself and preparing for your own assessment. The PE programme of study you have undertaken to prepare you for your role may have been provided by a university or under the auspices of a local partnership of employers and universities. It should have included teaching and promoted learning outcomes that, as a minimum, assist you in meeting the requirements of the PEPS Stage 1 (TCSW, 2013b). Local partnerships and universities offer this training in different ways – some training courses cover theoretical input that suffices for both Stage 1

and Stage 2 and the progression to Stage 2 is assessed via the supervision and assessment of a second student or another learner such as an NQSW (a combined pathway); other partnerships and universities offer additional 'Stage 2' courses and taught input prior to working with a second student or learner.

» Further personal study, reading and reflection, prior to submission for your own assessment. After undertaking the PE course, many universities or local partnerships require that you evidence the achievement of Stage 1 learning outcomes (Domains A–C) via the completion of a portfolio, an academic assignment or written pieces of work or through another form of assessment activity. To fulfil these requirements, further personal study, reading and reflection beyond the course of initial training will be required, all of which are activities that contribute to your CPD. The academic assignment or written pieces of work within the submitted portfolio require that you critically discuss your development as a PE and that your theoretical learning and knowledge of the elements of the PE role is reflected in the narratives about your practice. Consideration of the critical questions at the beginning of each chapter can help you with this.

» Attendance at PE support groups, further training or development sessions, PE workshops, etc. Many employers and universities offer further and ongoing training, updating and development opportunities to PEs, often in the form of PE workshops or support groups. Participation within these groups or workshops and the engagement in professional debates with other PEs that such activities foster, also contribute to your CPD as a PE.

» Participation in professional networks and engagement in professional discussions. Many practitioners and PEs participate in team or agency 'shared learning' or 'peer learning' forums, encouraging debate and consideration of professional issues and policy and practice pertinent to the PE's area of professional social work practice. Beyond these more formal forums, as a PE you may also participate in less formal professional networks, such as participating in discussions in team meetings or with colleagues regarding new national or local policy initiatives or developments in social work practice. With regard to your role as a PE, you may seek advice and guidance from a Stage 2 mentor, a fellow PE or agency co-ordinator/workforce development contact in relation to a student issue, or discuss an issue with the student's tutor relating to the student's written work or practice. Further, within England and Scotland, there exist national professional networks for PEs – the National Organisation for Practice Teaching

England (NOPT – www.nopt.org) and the Scottish Organisation for Practice Teaching (ScOPT www.scopt.co.uk). These are membership organisations which promote a national voice and good practice for PEs and those involved in Practice Education. Membership of these organisations is free and they each provide a forum for discussion and dissemination of ideas and information relevant to PEs, along with annual conferences where PEs can meet to consider the latest practice and policy issues and share good practice. You may also be one of the growing numbers of professionals who participate in the sharing of learning and debate within 'virtual' networks or social media platforms such as Twitter or the TCSW's 'communities of practice'. The latter is open to TCSW members and hosts forum discussions relevant to particular spheres of practice, including Practice Education.

» Using supervision to enhance your practice as a PE. As has been discussed within this book, supervision is a key area for practitioners, students and PEs. For PEs supervision should be an arena where they can discuss their practice, both in relation to the development of learning relevant to the PE's area of professional social work practice and to their role as a PE. The usefulness of supervision – for identifying and discussing CPD and further training requirements – should not be underestimated.

» Liaising and partnership working with your local university; contributing to Social Work Qualifying Programmes and contributing to research or co-researching with academic partners. There are a number of ways PEs can contribute to Social Work Qualifying Programmes and by so doing, contribute to their own CPD. As a PE you may have been called upon to help facilitate your local university's Practice Assessment Panel; reading and assessing student portfolios or contributing to moderation processes. Such liaison and contributory activities provide opportunities for learning and development in the PE role. PEs have also contributed to their local social work programmes in other ways, through offering shadowing opportunities for students or by contributing to the *30 days skills development* that social work programmes are required to provide under the new placement structure for qualifying social work education outlined in Chapter 1. Liaison with your local university may also allow you opportunities for contributing to research or participating as co-researcher with academic partners.

» Ongoing reflection, personal study and further reading. Within your field of professional practice, and during your work with students, challenges and dilemmas of practice will regularly arise. You will need to respond to these through asking yourself key, critically reflective questions and engaging in further reading, reflection and personal study. Each chapter within this book has encouraged you to consider some 'critical questions' which encapsulate some of the challenges, dilemmas and complexity of the PE role in relation to the subject covered in the chapter and the various 'professional development prompts' throughout this book require you to review and reflect upon your practice as a PE.

» Seeking feedback from students on your practice. Universities will have a quality assurance system that usually requires student feedback on their placement, considering the processes of the placement and the skills of the PE. This is one of the avenues for feedback although, as has been noted throughout the book, seeking such feedback and responding to it should be an integral element of the placement and should infuse the learning and teaching endeavour of Practice Education.

» Direct observation of your practice with a student and responding to feedback. The direct observation of your practice is an essential ingredient of achieving both Stage 1 and Stage 2 of the PEPS (TCSW, 2013b) and provides a unique opportunity to reflect upon your skills and development as a PE and thus can contribute to your CPD. We turn to this in the next section.

» Moving into new areas of practice in relation to the learning and development of others. The PEPS (TCSW, 2013b) require that independent *off site PEs* are Stage 2 proficient. For PEs who have attained Stage 2, some feel that becoming an independent off-site PE is an area of work they wish to move into. Further, the drive to strengthen the quality of learning and development of NQSWs and other practitioners undertaking CPD development and learning has resulted in national guidance (TCSW and Skills for Care 2013c) regarding the role of the Practice Development Educator (PDE). The PDE is a registered social worker who takes responsibility for supporting, assessing and/or supervising social workers undertaking post-qualifying professional development and learning. Roles such as these – PDE or as an independent off site PE – offers career and professional development opportunities for PEs and can contribute further to their own CPD.

Preparing for your assessment at Stage 1 – meeting Domains A–C and considering the role of the direct observation of your practice

To complete Stage 1 of the PEPS (TCSW, 2013b), PEs are required to provide evidence of their achievements against learning outcomes in Domains A–C and the Values for

PEs and supervisors, and need to be observed in their practice *teaching, supervising and assessing a social work student against the PCF* (p. 4). The observer of the PE's practice must be a practitioner with Stage 2 status. In the authors' experience of teaching, supporting and assessing PEs at both Stage 1 and 2, the direct observation of their practice causes many PEs some initial anxiety. The direct observation of the student's practice is an essential part of the teaching, learning and assessment of the student (see Chapter 6) and 'when the boot is on the other foot' and the PE is the person being observed it is perhaps worth reflecting upon how it feels and how fears and worries might be addressed.

As with observation of the student's practice, a reminder of the purpose of the observation – that it is an opportunity for the PE to gain developmental feedback about their professional practice and discuss and reflect upon it with a peer/the observer – is a helpful starting point. Preparation and consideration of areas to be covered and Domains and Values to be addressed during the observation will also be required and can provide a focus for PE /observer planning. Local employer partnerships and assessment processes may vary but most will require consideration and completion of a direct observation report or pro-forma, and PEs will need to take account of particular partnership requirements regarding direct observations of their practice and evidencing of the achievement of Domains A–C for Stage 1.

The general guidance given below is developed from the guidance given by a local employer and partnership network (Greater Lancashire and Cumbria SWETN, 2013) in relation to the direct observation of the PE's practice.

> » A suitable observation of the PEs practice would be a formal, planned supervision session.
>
> » Observing practice would usually include four stages of development.
>
> > 1. Pre-planning and discussion between the PE and the observer
> >
> > > » The pre-observation planning and discussion should focus on preparation for the observation and is an opportunity for the PE and observer to identify particular aspects of practice, Domains A–C that might be demonstrated during the supervision session and on which the focus of the feedback might be. If a session plan/supervision agenda is available it could be given to the observer and used to form the basis of the discussion.
> > >
> > > » The PE will have agreed the observation date and session with the social work student prior to the session, explaining the purpose of their observation.

» The PE will make suitable arrangements (for example, where the observers will sit/position themselves) for the observation.

» The PE and observer will agree how student comments and feedback will be sought and will arrange and agree arrangements for debriefing/feedback after the observation.

2. The observation

» The session should resemble normal practice as far as possible. For example, observation of the following supervision sessions – or that incorporate the following – could be helpful in demonstrating Domains A–C.

» A supervision session prior to the mid-point of the placement, considering the student's progress so far and discussing further assessment issues requiring attention during the second half of the placement.

» A supervision session after a student direct observation, involving the PE and student in developmental feedback, the PE encouraging student reflection on their practice.

» The PE helping the student relate theory to practice, either directly or discussing the student's written work/assignments; the PE using one of the tools and models suggested in Chapter 4.

» The PE encouraging/helping the student reflect on practice, perhaps using the tools/models referred to in Chapter 8.

» A supervision session towards the end of placement, helping the student reflect and consider skills gained and learning needs for their next placement/as they move into practice.

3. Feedback/debriefing after the observation

» How and when feedback would be given should have been agreed between the PE and observer. It would be expected that the observation is discussed and constructive feedback given in line with good practice on giving feedback (see Chapter 4).

4. Responding to feedback and completion of the direct observation report/pro-forma

» The direct observation report would usually be completed after the discussion above. Most direct observation reports expect the PE to reflect upon their practice and the feedback they have been given.

» Feedback involves thought and attention – as Bogg and Challis (2013) remind us – *effective feedback relies on sensitivity and realism on the part of the giver and an open-mindedness and willingness to learn from the receiver* (p. 95). They suggest the following when receiving feedback on your practice.

> » Be explicit – make it clear what kind of feedback you are seeking and on what element(s) of your practice.
>
> » Be attentive – concentrate on what is being said and on what the other person wants you to know, not just on what you want to hear. Hear the positives as well as the challenges and constructive feedback.
>
> » Be aware – notice your own reactions, intellectual and emotional, note if you are rejecting particular elements of feedback or in relation to a particular activity or task and reflect on why this is the case.
>
> » Be silent (initially) – try and stop yourself from making an immediate response or considering a response until you have heard all of the feedback and considered the implications. If you feel you need to explain, wait until after the full feedback to consider and attend to all that has been said.

For PEs submitting for both stages there are further opportunities – and expectations – for fuller reflection upon the feedback and the impact on their future practice to be considered. PEs should have access to guided support from a mentor, on either an individual or group basis. Discussions with the mentor, colleagues or fellow PEs can be used to further reflect upon feedback and the implications for their ongoing development and performance as a PE, as can written critical reflections or assignments for their assessed portfolio.

Preparing for your assessment at Stage 2 – meeting Domain D and considering your effective continuing performance as a PE

In order to complete Stage 2 of the PEPS (TCSW, 2013b), PEs are required to provide evidence of their achievements in relation to *additional* learning outcomes in Domains B and C and the learning outcomes within Domain D. PEs submitting for Stage 2 can evidence their achievement of the learning outcomes in their work with either a social work student or another learner who is being assessed in relation to the PCF, for example an NQSW.

The expectations and requirements of Domain D suggest that, as a practitioner, the PE should be able to demonstrate critically informed practice and applied current knowledge within their area of social work practice (D:5). Domain D also presumes that the PE will be operating with greater understanding and clarity of the PE role; underpinned by a critical awareness of their professional development as a PE and their strengths and areas for development (D:1) and with an ability to critically reflect on feedback from observers, students and tutors (D:2). Domain D also requires that the PE appraises and evaluates their performance in the role (D:1; D:2); considers how they intend to maintain currency as a PE and also how they might transfer their skills and knowledge to different roles and work with different learners, such as NQSWs. Many employers are encouraging PEs, particularly those who have attained Stage 2, to become ASYE assessors, mentors and supervisors of NQSWs –'Practice Development Educators' (PDEs) of others – recognising that the skills and knowledge of PEs are relevant and can be applied to other contexts and those who are learning in a post qualifying professional context. As has been noted, moving into new areas of practice such as off-site PEs and PDEs can provide exciting opportunities for Stage 2 PEs to develop their learning and expertise further.

In line with the 'new' approach to CPD outlined, and the suggestions given previously regarding the range of learning activities that could inform the PE's CPD, it can be seen that PEs can make use of a range of informal and formal learning and professional development opportunities that can help to demonstrate their continuing learning and development in the PE role and also their ongoing development as a practitioner. Further, referring again to Lester's (1999) metaphor (see Chapter 4) and the aspiration for the practitioner to move from being a *map reader* to a *map maker*, the requirements of Domain D and Stage 2 of the PEPS (TCSW, 2013b) expect this of the PE. Developing and moving to being a *map maker* requires that the PE appraises and gauges their development in the role and that they can make an assessment of their current levels of knowledge and understanding as well as their future needs and their strategies for meeting them.

One of the critical questions at the beginning of this chapter invited the PE to consider what they want to achieve in their CPD and what their future direction may be. To do this it can be helpful for the PE to clarify their current development in the role and how they are meeting the requirements of Domain D. Undertaking a SWOT or SWOB analysis – analysing Strengths, Weaknesses, Opportunities and Threats (SWOT) or Barriers (SWOB) – as suggested by Adams and Sheard (2013), is a useful tool that can help with this personal and career planning.

Professional **development prompt**

1. Undertake your own SWOT or SWOB analysis in relation to your development as a PE and identify your:

Strengths – these can be personal and professional strengths you possess but also wider; the strengths within your team and the wider resources available to you and the student within your agency. Consider what has worked well for you as a PE; how you have utilised your skills and judged the success of your role; what have been your highlights and what have you learned; how have you responded to and incorporated feedback in your practice?

Weaknesses – here you should consider areas where you know you need additional support and development, or aspects of the PE role that caused you the most challenge or that you were the least comfortable with. Perhaps reading particular chapters in this book has heightened your awareness of areas of your practice or skills as a PE that you need to develop? You can also consider the impact of wider factors and resources that cause a weakness and impact on your work with students and development in the PE role.

Opportunities – think about the opportunities that exist for your personal and professional development in the PE role or in new and related roles, such as an NQSW mentor or assessor, an off-site PE. These opportunities may be also be linked to CPD opportunities and activities previously mentioned.

Threats/Barriers – what have been or might be the threats and barriers to your development as a PE; what 'gets in the way' and can hamper your learning and development? These may be workload-related issues, organisational or personal issues. Some of these threats and barriers may be the resulting impact of wider and external factors that are affecting your workload and/or team morale, or they may reside within your employing agency; for example, agency structures may not support or prioritise CPD.

Strengths	Weaknesses
• –	• –
• –	• –
• –	• –
• –	• –

Opportunities	Threats or Barriers
• –	• –
• –	• –
• –	• –
• –	• –

2. Consider on your own, or with a PE colleague, how you might overcome some of the weaknesses and threats/barriers you have identified. Here you might like to consider:

   » what could be your role and the role of others in this? (ie what can your employer offer via CPD opportunities or workload management; what strategies can you employ; for example, how could you manage and plan your workload priorities or how might you pursue your CPD priorities with your employer?

   » what are your support and professional networks? How might you utilise and develop the support available to you – within your team, agency and local university network? Where can you go for further training, resources and information to help your development and how can you bring this to the attention of your agency, via your own supervision and/or discussions with others?

Conclusion

This book is underpinned by the belief that PEs need to engage in rigorous self-evaluation and demonstrate openness to examination of their practice. In the same way that students undertake a 'learning journey' during the course of their placement and training, so does the PE throughout their career. Further, for a PE in particular, continual appraisal of their practice and championing of CPD gives weight to the maxim 'always be a learner' and provides a powerful message to the student about the importance of CPD and models good professional practice. It is recognised that these are busy and challenging times for all practitioners and, for those who are also PEs or who facilitate the learning, assessment or mentoring of others who are post qualified, such roles are usually taken in addition to their 'day jobs'. However, it is essential that PEs strive to maintain a focus on their own CPD – including the strategies they can use to enhance it and the support they can call upon to maintain it – as this will not only be of benefit to themselves but will also contribute to the development of the next generation of social workers.

Appendix 1: Sample supervision agreement

Date : _/_/_   Review Date: _/_/_

Student Social Worker: _____

Practice Educator: _____

1   _____ and _____ (Practice Educator) will meet
    on a fortnightly basis for formal supervision. This will be for a period of
    between 2 and 3 hours.

2   The session will take place in a private room at an agreed venue
    (_____).

3   _____ and _____ (Practice Educator) will be
    prompt for supervision and will try to keep cancellations to a minimum. If
    either party has to cancel, a satisfactory explanation should be given and
    the session rearranged as soon as possible.

4   Interruptions to supervision will only be accepted in situations which
    require an immediate response.

5   Supervision should be a process based on an open and honest interaction
    between both parties. Confidentiality will be respected in accordance with
    agency policy.

6   _____ and _____ (Practice Educator) will each
    prepare an agenda and this will be prioritised at the start of each session.

7   _____ and _____ (Practice Educator) will try
    to ensure that all work is carried out in an anti-discriminatory and anti-
    oppressive manner. Power issues will be openly acknowledged and
    addressed by both parties.

8   Work/tasks undertaken by _____ will be discussed during
    supervision. This may include deadlines for work and evaluation of work
    undertaken to date.

9   _____ (student) to provide _____ (Practice
    Educator) with a copy of his/her daily log prior to each supervision ses-
    sion (preferably typed).

10 Supervision will be a forum in which to identify and review _____'s
    learning needs _____ (Practice Educator) will support
    _____ by identifying opportunities to meet any identified
    gaps in _____'s learning.

11 _____ (Practice Educator) will assist _____ with his/her learning during supervision. Discussions will contribute to assessment and will provide evidence for the final report/portfolio.

12 _____'s practice will be discussed and reflected upon during supervision with reference to assessment criteria. Discussions will contribute to assessment and will provide evidence for the final report/portfolio.

13 If the Practice Educator is off-site, he/she will arrange regular three way meetings with the student and practice supervisor to discuss the student's progress. These meetings will be formally recorded.

14 Following discussion, if agreement or compromise cannot be reached on a given matter, advice and guidance will be sought from an appropriate third party ie line manager, tutor, practice learning co-ordinator.

15 _____ and _____ (Practice Educator) will formally record sessions. They will be typed and checked/signed by both parties and copies kept. NB: Supervision records may need to be provided to the tutor at mid-point review and/or in the case of any dispute may provide evidence of actions agreed and taken.

Signed _____ (Student)

_____ (Practice Educator)

Appendix 2: Honey and Mumford's learning styles

(Honey and Mumford, 1992)

Type	Best learn and motivated by	Particularly like	Learn least from	Particularly dislike
Activists	• new experiences, problems or opportunities • short spontaneous exercises, tasks and games • excitement, drama, crisis and a variety of diverse activities • being in the 'limelight', including chairing, leading and presenting • being allowed to generate ideas without the constraints of practicality, policy or resource implications • being involved in a difficult task • being involved with others • having a go (trying something for the first time)	• participating in new or novel experiences • tackling real problems • activities relating to future roles	• taking a passive role, being asked to stand back and not get involved • assimilating and analysing data • working on their own • being asked, before the learning event, to identify what they will learn and after the event, to appraise what they have learned • being too theoretical • being involved in repetitive activities • being asked to carry out instructions with little room for manoeuvre • being meticulous to detail	• formulating objectives • clarifying • regularity • imposed structure • direct teaching inputs where they are expected to be passive or to sit on the sidelines

Type	Best learn and motivated by	Particularly like	Learn least from	Particularly dislike
Reflectors	• being able to stand back, listen to and observe what is going on • thinking before acting, having time to prepare • carrying out research where they can investigate and assemble ideas • reviewing what has happened and what they have learned • being asked to produce carefully considered analyses • exchanging views with other people in a safe, structured environment • reaching decisions in their own time, without pressure and tight deadlines	• observing someone else • the opportunity to plan before action • the opportunity to analyse • reviewing • thinking things over • giving and getting feedback • receiving help from others	• being forced into the limelight, to take a lead • situations which require action without planning • short notice of an event they have to organise • being given insufficient data on which to base a conclusion • being given exact instructions of how things should be done • being pressurised by time limits or rushed from one activity to the next • having to take short cuts or do a superficial job	• performing without preparation
Theorists	• being offered (part of) a system, model, concept or theory • having time to explore associations and inter-relationships between ideas, events and situations	• a carefully prepared session • situations where participation is structured	• doing something without a context or apparent purpose • situations which emphasise emotions or feelings	• concentrating on one particular problem • the absence of a process of generalisation

Type	Best learn and motivated by	Particularly like	Learn least from	Particularly dislike
	• having the opportunity to question the rationale or logic behind something • being pushed intellectually • structured situations with a clear purpose • ideas and concepts that emphasise rationality and logic (even if they do not appear immediately relevant) • being asked to analyse before being asked to generalise • attempting to understand complex situations	• intellectual activities • considering the theory behind something	• unstructured activities and open-ended problem solving • being asked to decide something without consideration to policy, principle or concept • exploring something only superficially • subject matter which is not statistically validated, has unsound methodology, is insufficient in evidence to support arguments • situations where they feel different from the other learners	• activities which encourage ambiguity and uncertainty • ad hoc sessions
Pragmatists	• an obvious link between the subject matter and a problem • techniques for doing things with obvious practical advantages (eg how to save time, revise better, etc.)	• situations where the learning activity is not seen to be related to a recognisable, immediate, practical benefit	• situations where there is not practice or clear guidelines on how to do a task	• moving outside their present role • an absence of any link to reality

Type	Best learn and motivated by	Particularly like	Learn least from	Particularly dislike
	• an opportunity to try out and practise and get feedback from a person they consider to be a good practitioner themselves • a model which they can emulate • situations where they can see that what they are doing is applicable to their job situation • immediate implementation of what they have learned • Concentration on practical issues (eg actions, plans, recommendations, etc.)	• teachers who seem distant from reality	• situations where they cannot implement what they are learning • situations where there is no apparent reward for the learning activity	

Appendix 3: Roles and responsibilities of the off-site Practice Educator and Practice Supervisor

These guidelines are intended to clarify roles in placements where there is an off-site Practice Educator and a Practice Supervisor, and to promote the benefits of this model. They are to be used flexibly and can be adapted to suit the particular placement setting.

Key:

PS = Practice Supervisor

OSPE = off-site Practice Educator

Expected tasks and roles of the Practice Supervisor

1. Daily operational responsibility.
2. Guidance for the student and OSPE on agency policies, procedures, intervention methods, case recording, etc.
3. Organising (with student) an induction programme.
4. Preparing the wider team and the line manager for the student placement; ensuring lines of accountability for the student's work.
5. Offering the student supervision on a formal and informal basis, and recording as agreed.
6. In conjunction with the OSPE facilitating learning opportunities to meet identified needs and assessment framework requirements.
7. Allocating work appropriate to individual student need and assessment framework requirements.
8. Dealing with routine student issues.
9. Maintaining communication with the student and the OSPE.
10. Maintaining oversight of health and safety procedures in respect of the student.
11. Undertaking direct observation of the student's practice and obtaining other feedback as appropriate from the placement setting, including from service users where appropriate (shared with OSPE).
12. Verifying and validating the student's practice examples and evidence.
13. Contributing to the final report.
14. Identifying his/her own learning and training needs.

15. Actively seeking professional development around the supervisory role and making use of available support and supervision both within the work setting and from the staff development section.

Expected tasks and roles of the off-site Practice Educator

1. Offering formal, regular supervision and recording as appropriate.
2. Planning for, monitoring and reviewing the learning needs of the student.
3. Maintaining an overview of the provision of learning opportunities and providing support to ensure the PS is able to meet placement requirements.
4. Developing his/her own knowledge and awareness of the student and the placement setting.
5. Focusing on assessment framework.
6. Offering education and guidance for the student on anti-oppressive practice, reflective practice, social work theory, transferable social work skills, the role of the social worker, etc., as well as on preparation of the portfolio.
7. Reading the student's reflective log and giving feedback.
8. Reviewing the evidence for the portfolio.
9. Undertaking direct observation of the student's practice and obtaining other feedback as appropriate from the placement setting, including from service users where appropriate.
10. Maintaining an overview of the student's written work, including sight of files/case notes/letters, etc.
11. Providing support to the student around the written assignments and co-marking with the tutor as required.
12. Taking responsibility for the final assessment decision and completing the final report with a contribution from the PS.
13. Maintaining communication with the PS; for example sharing supervision notes, attending three-way meetings.
14. Identifying his/her own training and learning needs.
15. Actively seeking professional development around the supervisory role and making use of available support.

Tasks to be undertaken by both Practice Supervisor and off-site Practice Educator

1. Attending the Learning Agreement meeting to set out responsibilities, placement expectations, student needs and practice experience.

2. Scheduling and attending a (recommended) minimum of three x three-way meetings to review the student's progress against agreed objectives.

3. Recording all meetings/discussions.

4. Validating practice examples.

5. Maintaining regular contact via agreed methods.

(Adapted from the *UCLan Practice Learning Handbook*, 2012, p. 16 – most universities will have procedures based on similar principles)

References

Adams, J and Sheard, J (2013) *Positive Social Work: The Essential Toolkit for NQSWs*. St Albans: Critical Publishing

Akhtar, F (2013) *Mastering Social Work Ethics and Values*. London: Jessica Kingsley Publishers

Bandura, A (1986) *Social Foundations of Thought and Action: A Social Cognitive Theory*. Englewood Cliffs, NJ: Prentice Hall

Barnett, R and Coate, K (2005) *Engaging the Curriculum in Higher Education*. Berkshire: SRHE and OUP

Bartoli, A, Kennedy, S, and Tedam, P (2008) Practice learning: Who is failing to adjust? Black African student experience of practice learning in a social work setting. *Journal of Practice Teaching & Learning*, 8(2): 75–90

Basnett, F and Sheffield, D (2010) The Impact of Social Work Student Failure upon PEs. *British Journal of Social Work*, 40(7): 2119–36

Beverley A and Worsley, A (2007) *Learning and Teaching in Social Work Practice*. Hampshire: Palgrave

Biggs, J (2007) *Teaching for Quality Learning at University*. Buckingham: SHRE and OU

Bogg, D and Challis, M (2013) *Evidencing CPD: A Guide to Building your Social Work Porftfolio*. St Albans: Critical Publishing

Borton, T (1970) *Reach, teach and touch*. London: McGraw Hill

Boud, D, Keogh, R and Walker, D (eds) (1985) *Reflection. Turning Experience into Learning*. Kogan Page: London

Brandon, J and Davies, M (1979) The Limits of Competence in Social Work: The Assessment of Marginal Students in Social Work Education. *British Journal of Social Work*, 9(3): 295–347

British Association of Social Workers (BASW) (2012) *The Code of Ethics for Social Work*. Online, available at: http://cdn.basw.co.uk/upload/basw_112315-7.pdf [Accessed 6 January 2014]

Brockbank, A and McGill, I (2007) *Facilitating Reflective Learning in Higher Education*. Berkshire: McGraw Hill

Brodie, I and Williams, V (2013) Lifting the lid: Perspectives on and Activity within Student Supervision. *Social work Education: The International Journal*, 32(4): 506–22

Brown, A and Bourne, I. (1996) *The Social Work Supervisor*, Buckingham: Open University Press

Burgess, R, Phillips, R and Skiner, K (1998) Practice placements that go wrong. *Journal of Practice Teaching*, 1(2): 48–64

CCETSW (Central Council For Education and Training in Social Work) (1989) *Improving Standards in Practice Learning: Regulations and Guidance for the Approval of Agencies and the Accreditation and Training of Practice Teachers, Paper 26.3*, London: CCETSW

Cartney, P (2000) Adult Learning Styles: Implications for practice teaching in social work. *Social Work Education*, 19(6): 609–26

Cartney, P. (2004) How academic knowledge can support practice learning: A case study of learning styles. *Journal of Practice Teaching and Learning*, 5(2): 51–72

Childrens Workforce Development Council (CWDC) (2009) *NQSW: guide for supervisors: newly qualified social worker pilot programme 2009–2010*. Online, available at: dera.ioe.ac.uk/id/eprint/11248 [Accessed 6 January 2014]

Clouder, L (2000) Reflective Practice: Realising its Potential. *Physiotherapy*, 86(10): 517–21

Collingwood, P (2005) Integrating theory and practice: the three-stage theory framework. *Journal of Practice Teaching in Health and Social Work*, 6(1): 6–23

Collingwood, P, Emond, R and Woodward, R (2008) The Theory Circle: A tool for learning and for practice. *Social Work Education*, 27(1): 70–83

Cree, V (2005) Students learning to learn in Burgess, H and Taylor, I (eds) (2005) *Effective Learning and Teaching in Social Policy and Social Work*. London: Routledge Palmer

Cree, V and Macaulay, C (2000) *Transfer of Learning in Professional and Vocational Education*, London: Routledge

Davys, A and Beddoe, L (2010) *Best Practice in Professional Supervision*. London: Jessica Kinglsey.

Davys, A and Beddoe, L (2009) The Reflective Learning Model: Supervision of Social Work Students. *Social Work Education: The International Journal*, 28(8): 919–33

Department for Education (DfE) (2009) *Building a safe and confident future – The final report of the Social Work Task Force*. London: Department for Education

Department for Education (DfE) (2010) *Building a safe and confident future: One year on*. London: Department for Education

Department of Health (2002) *Requirements for Social Work Training*. London

Doel, M, Shardlow, S, Sawdon, C and Sawdon, D (1996) *Teaching Social Work Practice*. Hants: Arena

Doel, M, Sawdon, C and Morrison, D (2002) *Learning, Practice and Assessment* London: Jessica Kingsley

Doel, M (2006) *Effective practice learning in local authorities (1): Strategies for improvement*. Leeds: Practice Learning Taskforce, Skills for Care

Doel, M (2010) *Social Work Placements: A Traveller's Guide*. London: Routledge

Douglas, H (2008) Preparation for contact: An Aid to Effective Social Work Intervention. *Social Work Education*, 27: 380–9

Dove, C and Skinner, C (2010) Early placement breakdown in social work practice placements. *Journal of Practice Teaching & Learning*, 10(1): 59–74

Duffy, K (2003) Failing students: a qualitative study of factors that influence the decisions regarding assessment of students' competence in practice. Caledonian Nursing and Midwifery Research Centre, School of Nursing, Midwifery and Community Health, Glasgow Caledonian University. Online, available at: http://www.nmc-uk.org/aFrameDisplay.aspx?DocumentID=1330

Edmondson, D. (2013) *Social Work Practice Learning: A student guide*. London: Sage

Eraut, M (1994*) Developing Professional Knowledge and Competence*. London: Falmer Press

Evans, D (1999) *Practice Learning in the Caring Professions*. Hants: Ashgate

Fernandez, E (1998) Student perceptions of satisfaction with practicum learning. *Social Work Education: The International Journal*, 17(2): 173–201

Finch, J (2011) Good Practice When working with Struggling or Failing Students. In *Welsh Organisation of Practice Teachers Annual Conference*. 10th November 2011. Welsh Organisation of Practice Teachers. Online, available from www.wopt.co.uk/conference.html [Accessed 12 February 2014]

Finch, J and Taylor, I (2013) Failure to Fail? Practice Educator's Emotional Experiences of Assessing Failing Social Work Students. *Social Work Education: The International Journal*, 32(2): 244–58

Fook, J (2002) *Critical Theory and Practice*. Sage: London

Ford, K and Jones, A (1987) *Student supervision*. London: Macmillan

Fraser, S and Matthews, S (eds) (2012) *The Critical Practitioner in Social Work and Health Care*. Sage: London

Furness, S and Gilligan, P (2004) Fit for Purpose: Issues from Practice Placements, Practice Teaching and the Assessment of Students' Practice. *Social Work Education*, 23(4): 465–49

Furness, S (2012) Gender at Work: Characteristics of 'Failing' Social Work Students. *British Journal of Social Work*, 42(3): 480–99

Gardiner, D (1989) *The Anatomy of Supervision: developing learning and professional competence for social work students*. Milton Keynes: SRHE and OUP

General Social Care Council (GSCC) (2002) *Code of Practice for Social Care Workers*. London: GSCC. Online. Available at: www.gov.im/lib/docs/socialcare/services/Codes_of_Practice.PDF [Accessed 7 January 2013]

GSCC (2005) *Post-Qualifying framework for social work education and training*. London: GSCC.

GSCC (2009) *Raising standards: Social work education in England 2007–8*. London: General Social Care Council

GSCC (2010) *Codes of Practice for Social Care Workers*. London: GSCC. Online. Available at: www.skillsfor-care.org.uk/developing_skills/GSCCcodesofpractice/GSCC_codes_of_practice.aspx

Gibbs, G (1988) *Learning by Doing: A Guide to Teaching and Learning Methods*. Oxford: Further Education Unit, Oxford Polytechnic

Gibson, M (2012) Narrative Practice and Social Work Education: The International Journal: Using a Narrative Approach in Social Work Practice Education to Develop Struggling Social Work Students, *Practice: Social Work in Action*, 24(1), pp. 53–65

Gilligan, P (2003) 'It isn't discussed'. Religion, belief and practice teaching: missing components of cultural competence in social work. *Journal of Practice Teaching*, 5(1): 75–95

Greater Lancashire and Cumbria Social Work Education Network (SWETN), (2013) *Assessment of Portfolio for Practice Educators*

Handy, C (1991) The Future of Work in a Changing World, Aurora Online, issue 1991. Online, available at: http://aurora.icaap.org/index.php/aurora/article/view/52/65 [Accessed on 13 November 2013]

Harden, RM and Crosby, JR (2000) The good teacher is more than a lecturer. *Medical Teacher*, 22(4): 334–47

Hawkins, P and Shohet, R (2006), *Supervision in the Helping Professions* 3rd edition. Berkshire: Open University Press

HCPC (2012a) *Standards of proficiency – Social Workers in England*. London: HCPC. Online, available at: www.hpc-uk.org/publications/standards/index.asp?id=569 [Accessed 4 September 2013]

HCPC (2012b) *Standards of conduct, performance and ethics*. London: HCPC. Online, available at: www.hpcuk.org/aboutregistration/standards/standardsofconductperformanceandethics/ [Accessed on 4 September 2013]

HCPC (2012c) *Standards of Continuing Professional Development (CPD)*. London: HCPC. Online, available at: www.hpc-uk.org/aboutregistration/standards/cpd/ [Accessed on 19 August 2013]

HCPC (2012d) *Guidance on conduct and ethics for students*. London: HCPC

HCPC (2012e) *Standards of Education and Training*. London: HCPC. Online, available from: www.hpcuk.org/assets/documents/1000295EStandardsofeducationandtraining-fromSeptember2009.pdf [Accessed 11 November 2013]

Heron, J (1975) *Six-Category Intervention Analysis*. Guildford: University of Surrey

Hinchcliffe, S (2009)*The Practitioner as Teacher* W.B. Saunders

Home Office (2012) *Equality Act 2010*. Online, available at: www.homeoffice.gov.uk/equalities/equality-act/ [Accessed 3 February 2013]

Honey, P and Mumford, A (1992) *The Manual of Learning Styles*. Maidenhead: P.Honey

Hughes, R (2006) *From Solos to Symphonies: Orchestrating Learning through Collaboration*. Campus Compact. Online, available at: www.compact.org/20th/read/from_solos_to_symphonies [Accessed 28 December 2007]

Jarvis, P and Gibson, S (1997) *The Teacher, Practitioner and Mentor in Nursing, Midwifery, Health Visiting and the Social Services* (2nd edition). Cheltenham: Nelson Thornes

Johns, C (2000) *Becoming a Reflective practitioner*. Oxford: Blackwell

Kadushin, A (1976) *Supervision in Social Work*. New York: Columbia University Press

Kennedy, S (2013) White woman listening, in Bartoli, A (ed) (2013) *Anti-racism in Social Work Practice*. St Albans: Critical Publishing

Kinman, G and Grant, L (2011) Exploring Stress Resilience in Trainee Social Workers: The Role of Emotional and Social Competences. *British Journal of Social Work* (2011) 41(2): 261–75

Knight, P (2006) The local practices of assessment in Assessment and Evaluation. *Higher Education*, 31(4):435–52

Knott, C and Scragg, T (2010) *Reflective Practice in Social Work* (2nd edition). Exeter: Learning Matters

Knowles, M. (1990) *The Adult Learner – a neglected species* (4th edition). London: Gulf Publishers

Kolb, DA (1984) *Experiential learning: experience as the source of learning and development*. Englewood Cliffs, NJ: Prentice Hall

Koprowska, J (1999) *Facts, Feelings and Feedback: A collaborative model for direct observation*. University of York

Lawson, H Inside the Long-Arm Model of Practice Teaching: The Experiences of Students, Practice Teachers and On-site Supervisors, in Lawson, H (ed) (1998) *Practice Teaching – Changing Social Work*. London: Jessica Kingsley

Lawson, H (2013) *Guide to the Professional Capability Framework and the Assessed and Supported Year in Employment*. Guides. Community Care Inform. Online, available at: www.ccinform.co.uk/articles/2013/02/11/7474/guide+to+the+professional+capability+framework+and+the+assessed+and+supported+year+in.html [Accessed 18 March 2013]

Lefevre, M (2005) Facilitating Practice Learning and Assessment: The Influence of Relationship. *Social Work Education*, 24(5): 565–83

Lester, S (1999) From map-reader to map maker: approaches to moving beyond knowledge and competence, in O'Reilly, D, Cunningham, L and Lester, S (eds) (1999) *Developing the Capable Practitioner: Professional Capability Through Higher Education*. London: Kogan Page

Lishman, J (2012a) Untitled. In *Failing to Fail? Best Practice event – working alongside Marginal and failing Social Work Students in a Practice Learning Setting*. (16 February 2012, pp.1–12). University of Chester Social Work Department. The Higher Education Academy, Online, available at: www.heacademy.ac.uk/assets/documents/events.trans_Lishman_DW079_Chester.pdf [Accessed 1 January 2013]

Lishman, J (2012b) *Retention and Success in Social Work Education*. York: Higher Education Academy. Online, available at: www.heacademy.ac.uk/resources/detail/retention/Lishman_social_work_report [Accessed 11 June 2013]

Lomax, R, Jones, K, Leigh, S, Gay, C (2010) *Surviving Your Social Work Placement*. Basingstoke: Palgrave Macmillan

Laming, Lord (2003) *The Victoria Climbié Inquiry Report*. Crown copyright

Laming, Lord (2009) *The Protection of Children in England: A Progress Report*. Crown Copyright

McKitterick, B (2012) *Supervision*. Berkshire: Open University Press

Maclean, S (2010) *The Social Work Pocket Guide to Reflective Practice*. Lichfield: Kirwin Maclean Associates Ltd

Maclean, S, Caffrey, B (2009) *Developing a Practice Curriculum*. Rugeley: Kirwin Maclean Associates Ltd

Maclean, S and Lloyd, I (2008) *Developing Quality Practice Learning in Social Work: A Straightforward Guide for Practice Teachers and Supervisors*. Rugeley: Kirwin Maclean Associates Ltd

Maclean, S, and Lloyd, I (2013) (2nd edition) *Developing Quality Practice Learning in Social Work: a Straightforward Guide for Practice Educators and Placement Supervisors*, Lichfield: Kirwan Maclean Associates Ltd

Marsh, S, Cooper, K, Jordan, G, Scammell, J and Clark, V (Undated) *Assessment of Students in Health and Social Care: Managing Failing Students in Practice, Making Practice-Based Learning Work*. Bournemouth University, Poole Primary Care NHS Trust and Royal Bournemouth and Christchurch Hospitals NHS Trust. Online, available at: http://shsmentor.swan.ac.uk/Documents/6%20Failing%20to%20Fail%2024%20 09%2008/entries%20in%20text/NHS%20interdisciplinary%20guidance.pdf [Accessed 12 June 2013]

Marton, F and Saljo, R (1976) On qualititative differences in learning: 1. Outome and process. *British Journal of Educational Psychology*, (46): 4–11

Moriarty, J, MacIntyre, G, Manthorpe, J, Crisp, B, Orme, J, Green Lister, P, Cavanagh, K, Stevens, M, Hussein, S and Sharpe, E (2010) My Expectations Remain the Same. The Student Has to be Competent to Practice': Practice Assessor Perspectives on the New Social Work Degree Qualification in England. *British Journal of Social Work*, 40(2): 538–601

Morrison, T (2001) *Staff Supervision in Social Care*. Brighton: Pavilion Publishing

Morrison, T (1993) *Staff Supervision in Social Care*. Brighton: Pavilion Publishing

Morrison, T and Wonnacott, J (2010) *Supervision: Now or Never. Reclaiming Reflective Supervision in Social Work*. Online, available at: www.local.gov.uk/c/document_library/get_file?uuid=d4830a8e-5e1d-466b-a48b-572b210b5ff8&groupId=10171

Munro, E (2011) *The Munro Review of Child Protection: Final Report – A child centred system*. DfE

NOPT (2013) *Code of Practice for PEs*. Online, available at: www.nopt.org/college-of-social-work-consultation [Accessed on 11 June 2013]

O'Sullivan, T (2010) *Decision making in social work* (2nd edition). Hampshire: Palgrave Macmillan

Oko, J (2008), *Understanding and Using Theory in Social Work*. Exeter: Learning Matters

Parker, J (2010a) When Things Go Wrong! Placement Disruption and Termination: Power and Student Perspectives. *British Journal of Social Work*, 40: 983–99

Parker, J (2010b) *Effective Practice Learning in Social Work*. Exeter: Learning Matters

Practice Learning Taskforce, Department of Health and Skills for Care (2006) *Capturing the Learning*. London

Quality Assurance Agency for Higher Education (2008), Subject Benchmark statement: Social Work, London: QAAHE. Online, available at: www.qaa.ac.uk/Publications/InformationAndGuidance/Pages/Subject-benchmark-statement-Social-work.aspx [Accessed 7 January 2014]

Race, P (2007) *The Lecturer's Toolkit: A practical guide to Assessment, Learning and Teaching* (3rd edition). Abingdon: Routledge

Rogers, J (1989) *Adults Learning* (3rd edition). Buckingham: OUP

Rolfe, G, Jasper, M, Freshwater, D (2011) *Critical reflection in Practice* (2nd edition). London: Palgrave Macmillan

Schon, D (1983) *The Reflective Practitioner*. London: Temple Smith

Shapton, M (2006) Failing to fail students in the caring professions: Is the assessment process failing the professions? *Journal of Practice Teaching & Learning*, 7(2): 39–54

Sharpe, M (2000) The assessment of incompetence: Practice teachers' support needs when working with failing DipSW students. *Journal of Practice Teaching*, 2(3), pp.5–18

Skills for Care (SfC) (2009) Draft Practice Educator Framework. Online [no longer available]

Smith, MK, (1999, 2008). 'Informal learning' in *The encyclopaedia of informal education*. Online, available at: http://infed.org/mobi/informal-learning-theory-practice-and-experience [Accessed 19 June 2013]

Social Care Institution for Excellence (2013) *Co-production in social care: what is it and how to do it.* London: SCIE

Social Work Reform Board (SWRB) (2011a) *Improving the quality and consistency of initial qualifying social work education and training*. London: Department for Education. Online, available at: www.collegeofsocialwork.org/uploadedFiles/TheCollege/Media_centre/Improving%20the%20quality%20and%20consistency%20of%20initial%20qualifying%20social%20work%20education%20and%20training%20final.pdf [Accessed on 10 June 2012]

Social Work Reform Board (SWRB) (2011b) *Effective partnership working*, London: Department for Education. Online, available from http://webarchive.nationalarchives.gov.uk/20131027134119/http://www.education.gov.uk/swrb/employers/a00198613/partnership-principles [Accessed 8 February 2014]

Social Work Reform Board (SWRB)/Local Government Association (undated) *Standards for Employers of Social Workers in England and Supervision Framework*. Online, available at: www.local.gov.uk/c/document_library/get_file?uuid=7e6d2140-fc0e-47cd-8b2f-2375812700ad&groupId=10171

Shardlow, S and Doel, M (1996) *Practice Learning and Teaching*. Hampshire: Macmillan Press

Taylor, C and White, S (2000) *Practising Reflexivity in Health and Social Welfare: Making Knoweldge*. OUP

Tedam, P (2012) The MANDELA Model of Practice Learning: An Old Present in New Wrapping? *Journal of Practice Teaching and Learning*, 11(3)

Shardlow, S and Doel, M (1996) *Practice Learning and Teaching*. Hampshire: Macmillan Press

The College of Social Work (TCSW) and the Higher Education Academy (HEA) (2012a) *Assessing Practice Using the Professional Capabilities Framework*. London: TCSW. Online, available at: www.tcsw.org.uk/uploadedFiles/TheCollege/Resources/Assessing%20practice%20using%20the%20PCF%20guidance%20Oct12(3).pdf [Accessed 6 January 2014]

TCSW (2012b) *Professional Capabilities Framework (PCF)*. London: TCSW. Online, available at:.www.tcsw.org.uk/pcf.aspx [Accessed 6 January 2014]

TCSW (2012c) *Understanding what the different levels mean*, v.2 November 2012. London: TCSW. Online, available at: www.collegeofsocialwork.org/uploadedFiles/PCFNOVUnderstanding-different-PCF-levels.pdf) [Accessed on 19 August 2013]

TCSW (2012d) *Domains within the PCF*, London: TCSW. Online, available from www.tcsw.org.uk/understanding-the-pcf [Accessed 15 February 2014]

TCSW (2012e) Practice Learning Guidance, *Placement Criteria*. London: TCSW. Online, available at: www.tcsw.org.uk/uploadedFiles/TheCollege/_CollegeLibrary/Reform_resources/PlacementCriteria(edref9).pdf [Accessed 6 January 2014]

TCSW (2012f) *Mapping of the PCF against the SoPs – June 2012*. London: TCSW. Online, available at: www.tcsw.org.uk/uploadedFiles/PCFNOVFinal Mapping of the PCF against the SoPs(1).pdf [Accessed 6 January 2014]

TCSW (2012g) *Endorsement of Qualifying Social Work Programmes: An Information and Guidance Booklet for HEIs*. London: TCSW. Online, available at: www.tcsw.org.uk/uploadedFiles/TheCollege/Media_centre/InformationandGuidanceforHEIs.pdf [Accessed 6 January 2014]

TCSW (2012h) *Professional Capability Framework – End of First Placement Level Capabilities*. London: TCSW. Online, available at: www.tcsw.org.uk/uploadedFiles/PCFNOVEndofFirstPlacementCapabilities.pdf [Accessed 6 January 2014]

TCSW (2012i) *Professional Capability Framework – Qualifying Social Worker Level Capabilities*. London: TCSW. Online, available at: www.tcsw.org.uk/uploadedFiles/PCF%20NOV%20Last%20Placement-QualifyingLevelCapabilities.pdf [Accessed 6 January 2014]

TCSW (2012j) *The Future of Continuing Professional Development*. London: TCSW. Online, available at: www.tcsw.org.uk/uploadedFiles/TheCollege/Media_centre/The%20Future%20of%20Continuing%20Professional%20Development%20-%20final%20paper%20for%20cpd%20AIG.PDF [Accessed 6 January 2014]

TCSW (2012k) *Effective Partnership Working*. London: TCSW. Online, available at: www.collegeofsocial-work.org/professional-development/partnership/ [Accessed 8 November 2013]

TCSW (2012l) Practice learning guidance, *'Developing skills for practice' and assessment of 'Readiness for direct practice'* (edref10). London: TCSW. Online, available at: www.tcsw.org.uk/uploadedFiles/TheCollege/_CollegeLibrary/Reform_resources/DevelopingSkillsReadiness(edref10).pdf [Accessed 6 January 2014]

TCSW (2012m) *Understanding what is meant by holistic assessment*. London: TCSW. Online, available at: http://www.tcsw.org.uk/uploadedFiles/TheCollege/_CollegeLibrary/Reform_resources/holistic-assessmentASYE1.pdf [Accessed 7 January 2014]

TCSW (2013a) *Code of Ethics for membership of the College of Social Work*. London: TCSW. Online, available at: www.tcsw.org.uk/uploadedFiles/TheCollege/Members_area/CodeofEthicsAug2013.pdf [Accessed 6 January 2014]

TCSW (2013b) *Practice Educator Professional Standards for Social Work*, London: TCSW. Online, available from www.tcsw.org.uk/uploadedFiles/TheCollege/Social_Work_Education/PEP%20standardsand%20guidance%20update%20proofed%20and%20final%20020021213.pdf [Accessed 8 February 2014]

TCSW and Skills for Care (2013c) *Social Work Practice Development Educators Guidance and Learning Outcomes*, London: TCSW. Online, available from www.skillsforcare.org.uk/Social-work/Social-work-CPD/Continuing-to-develop-social-workers.aspx [Accessed 8 February 2014]

TCSW/Higher Education Authority (HEA) (2012) *Holistic Assessment using the Professional Capabilities Framework Placement Assessment Report Template*. London: TCSW/Higher Education Academy. Online, available at: www.google.co.uk/url?sa=t&rct=j&q=&esrc=s&source=web&cd=2&ved=0CDsQFjAB&url=http%3A%2F%2Fwww.tcsw.org.uk%2FuploadedFiles%2FTheCollege%2FResources%2FAssessing%2520practice%2520using%2520PCF%2520-%2520assessor%2520report%2520October%25202012.doc&ei=jfTOUpv4GfHn7AbDvoBA&usg=AFQjCNHWHgh-dEji2H154BZMCYfuCVrTpQ&sig2=b_rFYXc-lhE675RAzfwUgg&bvm=bv.59026428,d.ZGU [Accessed 9 January 2014]

The International Federation of Social Workers (IFSW) (2012a) Statement of Ethical Principles. Online, available at: http://ifsw.org/policies/statement-of-ethical-principles [Accessed 6 January 2014]

The International Federation of Social Workers (IFSW) (2012b) *Definition of social work*. Online, available at: http://ifsw.org/policies/definition-of-social-work [Accessed 6 January 2014]

Thompson, N (1997) *Anti-Discriminatory Practice* (2nd edition). Basingstoke: Macmillan

Thompson, N (2006a) *Anti-Discriminatory Practice* (4th edition). London: Palgrave Macmillan

Thompson, N (2006b) *Promoting Workplace Learning*. Bristol: Policy Press

Thompson, N and Pascal, J (2011) Taylor and Francis online: Reflective practice: an existentialist perspective. *Reflective Practice: International and Multidisciplinary Perspectives*, Volume 12, Issue 1

Thompson, N, Osada, M and Anderson, B (1994) *Practice Teaching in Social Work*. Birmingham: PEPAR

TOPSS England (2002a) *The National Occupational Standards for Social Work*. Online, available at: www3.shu.ac.uk/HWB/placements/SocialWork/documents/SWNatOccupStandards.pdf [Accessed 7 January 2013]

TOPSS England (2002b) *Guidance on the Assessment of Practice in the Workplace*. Online, available at: www.google.co.uk/url?sa=t&rct=j&q=&esrc=s&source=web&cd=2&ved=0CDQQFjAB&url=http%3A%2F%2Fwww.wlv.ac.uk%2FDocs%2Fhlss-swpl-guid-prac-wkpl.doc&ei=HpgnUpHLIKuf7AbeioD4Cg&usg=AFQjCNFb1wdOX_lQBdHLxIZ9GbIJ_-LmDQ&bvm=bv.51495398,d.ZGU [Accessed 4 September 2013]

Trevithick, P (2005) *Social Work Skills: a practice handbook* (2nd edition). Berkshire: McGraw-Hill/Open University Press

Trevithick, P (2008) Revisiting the Knowledge Base of Social Work: A Framework for Practice. *British Journal of Social Work*, 38: 1212–37

Trevithick, P (2012) *Social Work Skills and Knowledge: A practice handbook* (3rd edition). Berkshire: McGraw Hill/OUP

Trotter, J and Gilchrist, J (1996) Assessing DipSW students: anti- discriminatory practice in relation to lesbian and gay issues. *Social Work Education*, 15(1): 75–82.

Tsui, M (2005) *Social Work Supervision: contexts and concepts*. London: Sage

UCLan (2012) *Practice Learning Handbook MA and BA Social Work 2013/14*. University of Central Lancashire

Wallcraft, J, Fleischmann, P and Schofield, P (2012) *The involvement of users and carers in social work education: a practice benchmarking study*. London: SCIE

Walker, J, Crawford, K and Parker, J (2008) *Practice Education in Social Work: A Handbook for Practice Teachers, Assessors and Educators*. Exeter: Learning Matters

Ward, T. (2002) *A Toolkit for Practice Teachers*. Scottish Organisation for Practice Teaching

Waterhouse. T, McLagan, S and Murr, A (2011) From Practitioner to Practice Educator: What Supports and What Hinders the Development of Confidence in Teaching and Assessing Student Social Workers? *Practice: Social Work Action*, 23(2): 95–109

Williams, S and Rutter, L (2010) *The Practice Educators Handbook*. Exeter: Learning Matters

Williams, S and Rutter, L (2013) *The Practice Educators Handbook* (2nd edition). Exeter: Learning Matters

Wilson, G, Walsh, T and Kirby, M (2008) Developing Practice Learning: Student Perspectives. *Social Work Education*, 27(1): 35–50

Wilson, G, O'Connor, E, Walsh, T and Kirby, M (2009) Reflections on Practice Learning in Northern Ireland and the Republic of Ireland: Lessons from Student Experiences. *Social Work Education: The International Journal*, 28(6): 631–6

Wonnacott, J (2012) *Mastering Social Work Supervision.* London: Jessica Kingsley

Wonnacott, J (2013) Supervision: a luxury or critical to good practice in times of austerity? (Conference presentation, 28 June 2013). Online, available at: www.in-trac.co.uk/news/supervision-in-times-of-austerity/, [Accessed 21 August 2013]

Wray, J, Fell, B, Stanley, N, Manthorpe, J and Coyne, E (2005) *The PedDs Project: Disabled Social Work Students and Placements.* University of Hull

Young, PH (1967) *The Student and Supervision in Social Work Education.* London: Routledge and Kegan Paul

Index